HOMOSEXUALITY

**Lesbians and Gay Men
in Society, History and Literature**

HOMOSEXUALITY

**Lesbians and Gay Men
in Society, History and Literature**

General Editor
JONATHAN KATZ

Editorial Board
Louis Crompton
Barbara Gittings
Dolores Noll
James Steakley

Research Associate
J. Michael Siegelaub

See last pages of this volume
for a complete list of titles

Either is Love

ELISABETH CRAIGIN

ARNO PRESS
A NEW YORK TIMES COMPANY
New York — 1975

Editorial Supervision: LESLIE PARR

———◆———

Reprint Edition 1975 by Arno Press Inc.

Copyright © 1937 by Harcourt, Brace
and Company, Inc.
Reprinted by permission of Harcourt
Brace Jovanovich Inc.

HOMOSEXUALITY: Lesbians and Gay Men in
Society, History and Literature
ISBN for complete set: 0-405-07348-8
See last pages of this volume for titles.

Manufactured in the United States of America

———◆———

Library of Congress Cataloging in Publication Data

Craigin, Elisabeth.
 Either is love.

 (Homosexuality)
 Reprint of the ed. published by Harcourt, Brace,
New York.
 1. Love. 2. Lesbianism--United States.
3. Homosexuality--Personal narratives. I. Title.
II. Series.
HQ76.C7 1975 176   75-12311
ISBN 0-405-07379-8

EITHER IS LOVE

Either is Love

ELISABETH CRAIGIN

HARCOURT, BRACE AND COMPANY

NEW YORK

Designed by Robert Josephy

PRINTED IN THE UNITED STATES OF AMERICA
BY QUINN & BODEN COMPANY, INC., RAHWAY, N. J.

EITHER IS LOVE

CHAPTER I

THE misfortune of this memoir is that it must be written in a vacuum. I should like to begin with an unshackled account of my husband, revealing to his public all the delightful part of him that never was generally known. But if there were no other restriction, an open tribute was a thing he abhorred. Though his special qualities were the ones that give eminence in his calling, his nature was of a kind not widely understood in our times. Selection was its key; enthusiasms had a minor place. He cared principally for what he could achieve in his field, his pleasures mostly subjective, his virtues unobserved by himself, and the recognition that came to him disdained when it was not disregarded. Part of his life was passed in a high office where he had authority in the lives of thousands, but the marketplace was never his home; his native element was seclusion. He had the widest sympathy, but discern-

3

ment was even more characteristic of him, and his judgment was regarded by his colleagues as something outside the common attainment of man. As he was no egoist the opinions men held of him did not work much into his consciousness. His prayer was that those whom he dealt with should be approachable through reason, not merely puppets of their feelings, and if this was so he could always make his way with them and ultimately bring about his ends. Only to a few was he deeply known, chiefly those who had worked the longest near him and were most acquainted with the color and movement of his mind, and those few gave him their all of admiring love. Their lives were relieved through the anodyne of his humor, the sudden unruffled kind of humor with great understanding just below it that can loosen and steady and weld a whole body of workers at once.

The marriage that we surprisingly made when I was in my late thirties, joining our so dissimilar lives and affairs, was a particularly, a very exceptionally successful one. It was not much known to the throng of his professional acquaintance, due to that instinct of his for retirement. Some of my own friends were a good deal puzzled by him, though those who waited for the moving of the waters were always rewarded. The spontaneous outpouring of sympathy that followed his death was therefore more concerned for me in my predicament at losing him than reflecting the reality of him with any general understanding. Some who did not know his private life guessed at it touchingly, however, and we had joint friends who appeared to have taken in the unity that existed between us as well as his own high achievements that were independent of me.

"My impression was that he was acquainted with the secret springs of life," one wrote. "The world loses with you a citizen of great value, of a rare kind, so upright and so cultured," said another. "I always thought he had that keen and sure sense of honor not often met with in these times," came from another. "All my life I have lived under the knowledge of what I owed him," wrote an early friend. "Such complete companionship as you had is so rare you must cling to that—a few years with him were better than a lifetime with most—" and the woman who said that knows something about making successful companionship out of unlikely materials. One man who was almost a stranger to us said, "I always felt that the noble and interesting traits that bound you together were a phenomenon apart." Unknown to us the binding had been noted, though the causes were not fathomed.

To be bound is to be bound. When this marriage was struck by the thunderbolt I had no insulation whatsoever and was completely at the mercy of the blow. All who are acquainted with grief know something of what the following months were like. The nights of aching, the struggle to escape from accomplished fact, the hunger for his return constantly renewed like stabs of pain, the mist of bewilderment pierced through every now and again with realization, the secondary losses in the wake of the primary one—all this experience is familiar to many. Yet if the binding has been a valid one, it does not finish with death. The human pairing continues in the mind and movements of the survivor. I am saturated, not with my husband's "memory" as it is called, but with the sense of his methods, of his reaction to events, his handling of problems, his inaccessiblity to trifles, his watchfulness for the active principle in ideas. The special work he was doing is full of emotion for me; I stalk its developments wherever I think they may be looked for. I need no substances to be in relation with his personality, not even his books; not the retelling of his stories nor the echo of his favorite expressions. He is nearer than that; a kind of transubstantiation in myself has taken place. Even our marked differences of habit or opinion do not separate us—they did not separate us in his lifetime. When I swing far out on my orbit away in space, his pull, like gravitation, brings me back to swing out as far perhaps on the other side. It may be that only I myself can recognize him in my behavior, but I know that allegiance is its prevailing wind, not allegiance to a set of principles founded on another's experience, but allegiance to the pride he has left in me.

Allegiance as his wife in the narrow sense is not of any importance. I could take another husband tomorrow without derogating in the slightest from loyalty to him. He would be the one to propose that course to me if I thought it would bring me satisfaction. He was far more than husband to me—he was an enveloping friendliness, a climate, a sunlight to my searching growth. But I may not turn on or off the will to wed, as I turn on or off the radio. We do not control these tendencies. The willingness to marry is based on profound inner causes, and they are not present in me save through recollection. It is now some time since he has been gone, and my involuntary nunnery is becoming a place of calm. My interest in people is detached rather than personal; electric messages no longer pass to me from outside. I can move more freely among men because of it; I can work and laugh and eat with men as from behind some invisible wall. These changes come; they are there. "I shall never tell you that, until there is not an inch left between us," he once wrote me early in our relations. Astonishing remark, so quiet and so threatening. It comes back to me now, when though his presence is removed to timeless distance there is not an inch left between us in this other sense, a sense he was not thinking of when he said it. Certainly no inch into which another personality could insert itself.

8

Either is Love

When we came together we were neither of us young. I was the seared survivor of an earlier passion. He had lost a beloved young wife in an unspeakable accident. Our gravitation toward each other was slow, and had phases of great pain for both of us before I finally saw in him my genuine mate. As often happens in second marriages, the relation began in sympathy—the acute sympathy I had for his cruel state after the accident. Sympathy was always a large part of our case. His was never-failing in any of my chronic difficulties. The love that sprang in us had its gradual boilings and recessions, gathering head as time went on. For my part the ebbing of the tide was always stronger than its on-coming, and these periods caused us both suffering. Through all of them his friendship never faltered, invariably generous, invariably kind, upholding me with steadfastness however much I stabbed him and discouraged him in the course of my disturbances.

A constant obstacle in our path was the war, making it thorny and uncertain, and full of absences prolonged almost to the breaking-point. Our love-making had lurid features. It appealed to the poetic imagination in both of us to continue grave and unquestioned participants in our respective and sober worlds, both of them rather wide worlds and in some sense public worlds, while our private relations contained the most uncanonical adventuring. For long I was not ready to believe that we could make a successful marriage. I was too often out of love with him. My heart, as I told him, would rush away from him back to a draughty ill-lit room in a nearly abandoned house, where love did know its maximum of joy and happiness, in the face of illness and uncertainty and all the troubles in the calendar. The truth was, I thought, that I could never love again like that. But I was mature; I felt my feet securely on the ground, and certainly his were. I needed some of the things that he could give me, whether or not we should ever completely marry, and he understood that well. He took pride in being able to minister to my need in a passionate friendship governed by self-control. It was that self-control that conquered me in the end, extraordinary as it was. Our letters show something of our debate as to whether such a thing was really possible. I wanted convincing.

Either is Love

"Give yourself to me, darling," he would write. "I'll not accept you, not till I can do it decently and in honor. But you can let go all the same—leave yourself to me. I am able to remain continent while I love you. I wouldn't answer for myself if I didn't love you. You have all the lesser temptations crowded off the boards, and you are not so much a temptation as an aspiration. Of course I do have to keep the body under and that does involve physical strain. But I can't see how I am to measure the amount of that strain for your benefit except by telling you that I am equal to it."

"You differ from the average woman in more ways than one. You are more strongly sexed. It is probably one of the provisions that nature has made for the benefit of the race that women are colder as a rule than men. If they weren't, society would be dissolved in an orgy of lust. But you do not injure society because your inhibitions are in good working order. You have a useful brain and an efficient will. Nine out of ten women with your passions would be as promiscuous in their sexual affairs as men are, if they could command the opportunities of men. There are a lot of them who are."

Either is Love

It tempts me to recall more of these charming letters he wrote during the deep immersion of his wooing.

"These last three days I have been good for nothing but to make love to you. If you feel like 'Judgment to come' and your cold has aged you, that's what I ought to be doing. Not here a thousand miles away but where you are. You know how I can make you radiant by just loving you and making you conscious of the fact. But why make you radiant when I am not there to see? This morning, a dull showery dawn, a flicker was calling insistently in the distance, and I coming out of dreams where you were into the world where you are, possible for me only because it contains you, a wonderful two-legged creature with brains. I made love to you after that flicker waked me up this morning, oh most astonishingly. You missed something. All with talk. Of course I had you in my arms, but that was not important. I made you drunk with words. I'll show you. How is it to keep an aged common professional man all stirred up this way, dwelling amorously on you, aching over your weariness, just physically aching, my darling, wanting to shelter you from all the world, including himself."

"Do take care of yourself, my dear. I want you sick or well, fat or thin. I can see you a little haggard without being less attracted to you. Indeed you have a particular fascination for me when you look tired and drawn in the face. I don't care how bad you are either, God forgive me. I opine that I may still have discoveries to make about you, with the appalling certitude that whatever they are, I shall keep right on loving you. Old man Browning had a word for that, but what it is you will never guess, and I will not tell you."

"The truth is that your letter, all about heavenly weather, new clothes and such, has caused the old Nick to turn over in the grave where I interred him some time since. Not that I am all distraught because I can't see you in those new clothes. The real trouble is that clothes, especially quite lovely clothes —well, there is a kind of reverse English in my association of the concept clothes with the concept you. Ordinarily clothes are something to put on, and that is well enough, but when I think of your clothes—

"This perversion tends to dull a little my appreciation of the true beauty of new dresses. How surrender to the perfection of the hang of your dress over your person, when I can't help thinking how deliriously delightful it would be to hang it over the back of a chair."

"I hark back to that early visit now because it tested so completely our control of bodily desire. You were not my mistress when we parted that time, and whether you know it or not that is a considerable guaranty that my desire for you will never overbalance my love. You are not my mistress, but have I not undone the curiously located fastening of the ultimate flimsy silken excuse for clothing that covered my love and bared all her body to my enterprises? But she is still a spinster and not merely a technical spinster. To have you in my power, to realize vividly the joy that lies in the full use of that power, to have the temptation pounding in my temples and for the instant to refrain—it is an adventure worth while. Though not for always, my dear."

Either is Love

Though I had become emotionally ready, for the first time in my life, for a thoroughgoing sex life, I was in the greatest doubt whether allying myself completely to him would not be too complicated for good results. His theory, constantly recurred to, was that of course such a marriage as ours would be was chancy, but any marriage is that; that not marrying is also chancy, and life consists in taking chances. The art of life is in calculating the chances intelligently.

"I don't like waiting. To have you so very near me, yielding yet hesitant, poised as it seems sometimes to take flight, and to refrain from reaching out and taking you, substituting my will for your hesitations and fears, making you irremediably mine, is no light sport for me. A strange courtship, this of ours. Has it ever struck you how we reverse each other's procedure? My love for you commencing with admiration for your quick darting mind, the freedom and largeness of your spirit, your courage, loyalty and wise tenderness,—passion and desire coming later. You traveling with far more difficulty in quite the opposite direction. I shall never quite

15

master my bewilderment at that. It isn't that the idea of marrying me repelled you in the beginning— nothing surprising in that. But the attraction I had for you—how should you be cognizant of a lover in me when I hardly knew him myself? You tell me I am an amazing lover and I hug that testimonial to my bosom, but I am hardly less amazed than you. And when you doubtfully wonder if you haven't got me yet to learn, I suspect you are near the truth. I have myself to learn. You are constantly showing me to myself. I change, or at least I find myself increasingly as the days pass."

"Yes, I shall come back to you. You still tell me now and then that I am not your man. The time has not come for me to give the lie direct to that statement. But I tell *you* that you waste words. Of all the factors that enter into and complicate our approaching marriage,—I admit there are factors,— the least important is that opinion of yours that I am not your man. I mention the fact and pass on. Oneida—(he was on the train) there is where they tried to get rid of marriage but it didn't work; and now one gives Oneida spoons for wedding presents, or the advertisements say one does. And after all, my dear—how dear you are—marriage is not so perilous as one thinks. Marriage with me, I mean. I couldn't answer for any marriage where I wasn't leading man."

It was a little thing, as he expected, that caused the opening of the floodgates toward him, when I wrote him that I had gone to him in mind and would henceforth have no more doubts. It was seeing his picture suddenly, unexpectedly, in a magazine. I saw him there and instantly knew. Uncertainty was over. The heavens seemed to have opened and let fall a cooling relief. I asked only to be joined to him in all ways possible as soon as it could be done. I must have written him in wild abandon and joy. I must have asked, How did it happen?

"The clerk handed me your letter and I came back up here and sat with it, loving you, holding you, remembering every gracious curve and line of you. Dawn has found me still sitting here with you and your love-letter. What am I to say? The case demands words, being at this distance, and there are no words. If we were face to face—ah then—I could take you to me, molding your body to mine, with a gesture, several gestures in one, that would leave you no room for doubt of your belonging to me, no room for doubt and little room to breathe. Molding your body to mine, taking your lips, my God! your lips, slowly, one at a time. Holding you all the time shamelessly, boldly, this hand here and the other there, drawing you closer. And I must deal in words. Do not ask me, dear, how this happened. What I could most easily put in words is my lack of any reasoned understanding of that. When I apply my intelligence to that problem, I say it is out of all reason that you should come to me, glad to be taken that way. I think it my duty to warn you, to tell you to take thought. But deep under that, more valid, more powerful to control, has always been the conviction that sooner or later you would come to me, not to me but to the refuge of my love. Something this way I knew it would happen, some little trivial thing would awaken you to the knowledge of yourself and me. I think, dear woman, you have come so close to me now that I must grasp and hold you. I think I'll not humor your fluctuations as I

18

have in the past. If you try to run away I'll bring you back with a strong hand. You are open to me now, body and soul. I'll not let you shut yourself up. And I shall make demands upon you. There are so many things you must tell me, lying in my arms. Things you will not tell except in answer to repeated insistent peremptory questions. I am storing them up. I will lay your past as bare as your body. Then I shall have you all.

"And so I babble, with your dear rash love-letter nestling about my heart. You are going to marry me, are you? How often must I tell you to wait till you're asked. Do you expect to wear my resistance down by a process of attrition?

"Oh, this world is a fearful place, full of beauties— both aspects equally dazzling. How do we—how *do* we live them through?"

CHAPTER II

AFTER his death there came to me from an office of his a sealed suitcase black with dusty soot. When I got it open I found in it all my own early letters to him. Classified and ranged chronologically they were, dates on the outside of packets, with sometimes a small notation of the feeling between us at the time, or the matters at issue. I hardly stopped until I had devoured them all. His whole presence was reproduced for me as if I were writing him those letters afresh. The letters a man elicits from a woman are a monument to his powers. He had the technique to draw from me those responses as his physical touch drew me from myself. Much of it was hardly writing—it was ejaculation.

"You blessing! that is what I woke at dawn saying, your wonderful message from Wednesday between me and my sheet where it lay warm all night.

Either is Love

And all yesterday inside my 'shift.' Such a message
—its depth, its warmth, its intensity! It said that I
am your destined prey. It said you are stalking me,
that we belong to each other, it said that I seem to
you provocative, and other things to thrill and pos-
sess me. With a message like that against my heart
I ought to be fortified against a world of pin-pricking
discomforts. What emerges from six days of separation is that my youwardness is increased about four-
fold. I am a living flame of remembering, oh yes.
You have made yourself master of me, and anywhere
I tried to escape, there would be bonds holding me.
Bonds is a precious word. In my sleepy memory
certain inspired words of yours often float. 'Your
loving enemy.' 'Revealing you to me your loving
enemy.' To be in your power, and feel security
there, is a combination unsurpassed. To be robbed
of my will and have it kept safe for me, as dear to
you as to me. If nothing more ever comes to me
through you, I have had that."

"Oh, the beautiful marvelous device of sex! My
own ecstasy in being pliable and soft is dual, both
personal and vicarious. Yours in being masterful and

swift the same—you feel my delight for me as well as your own. How we two have lived beauty—no sacrifices, no immolation of one to the other, but mutual satisfying and giving! Our minds fit perfectly in this relation. Sex, the strange battle in which the woman always fiercely thirsts to lose! I love you to have taken down my defenses. To be sure I may be said to have invited their undoing, but not in any such measure as you have performed the service for me. Wonderful is the knowledge that I am defenseless to your imagination. Staying the while, for an indeterminate period, a thousand miles away, with my constant serious occupation, my friends coming and going, new acquaintances, etc., about me, and all the while, to your imagination, defenseless. If you could be here beside my bed in this solitude with only this one lamp in all the house burning—perfectly alone together—if it were only to be reading something together and you never even laid your hand on me, what a sweet enclosed communion it could be! But you would of course lay a hand on me. The divine threat of it! Your effect upon me so calculated, the coursing communication between us, and you so passive aboveboard, the healthy sexuality of you disguised under that disarming passivity, totally depraved angel that you are."

"*Délices*—how does our English language get on without that word? I often search for one to take its place, the noun for something more definite than delight and more subtle than our unsatisfactory word deliciousness. *Ivresse* is another. We have no word for the intoxication of the senses as such. But you can say things pretty well. 'Devising new ways of being gently indecent with you'—was ever a phrase more calculated to seduce? I let out a long sigh of rapture over it—the fullness of satisfaction in it! Make me feel your control of me all you will. It is my one pure happiness, my délices, the sense of being in bondage to you, waiting for you, waiting for you to claim what you will have, unable to draw apart from you, unable to close myself against you if you will have it otherwise. Are there storms in your body, dearest heart, parallel to the storms in mine? I believe it. Mine is an assortment of definite pains and aches which are nothing in the world but the cry of Eve for Adam. I know you will accord me the

right to be wedded to you at the very earliest opportunity. Even if final darkness does descend, some
one of all those final darknesses that hover over us,
I will have been made your own—I can wear you, I
will have the first rights to you. Best get the uncertainties over first of course, only during your work
upon the uncertainties repeat occasionally to yourself the formula, 'The girl, darn it, wants me!' I
don't know that I was born to be a fiancée; few
fiancées exhibit less coyness. I was born to be a mistress. But our joint prejudice in favor of a thin gold
ring will have first to be placated."

As I swept through the carefully ranged packets
in the suitcase I came upon a heartbreaking thing.
There was a little collection of small white envelopes
that were not from me, tightly sealed and bare of
superscription. In the upper corner of each was a
minute device in ink, apparently a date and some
tiny reminder intelligible only to himself. Hard
upon the trail of my dead, I broke one open. Out of
it slid a small drift of black paper-ash. Every white
envelope the same, twenty or thirty of them as full
as they would hold of ash. When during correspond-

ence I had given way to overheated rhapsody, I had evidently asked him to burn what I had said. Slipping from these envelopes was the evidence. I had trusted his faithfulness and he had complied in order to assure me I was safe, but in his tenderness he had not sacrificed so much as an ash. On the outside was the cipher of reference for himself. Later came to light the corresponding period in his own letters:

"This is an afternoon of burnt offerings, letters of yours, read over for the last time lingering, then placed in a copper brasier over an alcohol flame; curling, twisting there in agony like the living things they are, and finally shriveling to blackness shot here and there with red as a summer cloud is shot with lightning, red that gives place to the white of ashes. If they cannot live, this is the way for them to find their death, in leaping flames. I have to crumple them up to get them in the brasier. They relax and uncurl the moment they feel the heat. So I have felt your body loosen and grow lax.

"The suspense when I pick up a letter, as to whether it is destined to the flames, the disappointment in finding it sufficiently discreet and cool to be saved and the pleasure of not having to burn it, and then the fierce devastating joy of encountering a passage that is beyond pardon. Your letters so ineffably you, the passionate tempestuous you that your public and friends little dream of, that no one knows but me. The more they surrender you to me, the more certainly they cannot live. And I must be the agent of their destruction. Breathe freely about your letters to me, dear woman. The devouring flame has been through them and your good name is safe. Oh, it is a waste! A unique record, your letters. The first time perhaps in the history of the world, certainly in the history of our world, that a chaste passionate woman has so bared herself to a male friend. You don't know how clean this freedom that I have with you makes me feel. Now write me some more fuel."

My letters were not all amatory outpourings, far from it. They were the record of my days and difficulties, rushing to his understanding. He had a lively interest in all I was doing, and I talked at length with him of the questions involved in his own work. There was much interchange on what we read, which when possible we read together, one at each end of the line. And there was the anxious subject, after we thought of marrying, of how his occupation was possibly to be combined with the difficult elements that a wife and a ménage would bring to it. And all the while the war, more than one phase of the war which injected so much perplexity into our position. The correspondence was always bristling with problems, not the smallest of which was my own ever-recurring bad health which seemed, even after I loved him, to threaten our coming together more than any other one factor. And we did not always see things alike.

"We have a lot to talk about, yes indeed," he said. "I am not so restless about it as I have been. One thing that contributes to repose of spirit is my serene confidence in your rare wise forbearing tolerance. I feel that no misunderstanding need be final, no rash mistaken impulse fatal. If you do not divine all that is needful to clear matters up, you will always listen patiently to explanation. A quality not to be overvalued. Women are prone to forgiveness, they enjoy the superior position it offers; but they are not so capable of intelligent absolution."

He once sent me flowers inscribed "With best wishes and bold memories." It is a message that still starts the "prehensile gesture of my heart" toward him. His best wishes were very inclusive, not only for my pleasure but for other things. In one of his remarkable love-letters he said:

"I'm glad your body is a wonderful instrument of love, glad that I have been able to draw some harmonies from it that don't displease you. I think of new harmonies. But you are more to me than a lovely and amorous woman and always will be. What that more is I have never been able to tell you fittingly. I curse the poverty of language. Some of my letters to you have been ground and polished in a sort of agony to make them faithful messengers of my love, but they all fail more or less. . . . If you know enough of it to feel safe and exultant in it, that must serve for now. As for doing you good, being married to me is a discipline that couldn't fail to do good to the victim. It would do you good to learn to

28

look at things with my eyes as well as your own, not because you love me, but because I have rather good eyes, and your worst fault, so far as my present advices go, is a belief that your own eyes are all-sufficient. No, you don't proclaim that belief, you repudiate it, but it is there, in ambush, and it pops out at every turn of the road. However, I'm not marrying you to give you the use of another pair of eyes. I want you, and if I decently can I'll take you, and if there is anything in the two of us it will grow and bloom the better when we are together."

CHAPTER III

A MOST improvised sort of wedding was at length wrested from unwilling fate and we were together, but only for a few months. It had been long enough to prove the wisdom of what we had done. When we parted again something of our successful married fusion is evident in the correspondence which was our only bridge for so long once more.

"I could only get an upper berth," he wrote. "But I can accommodate the thought of you in an upper berth. It is one of my favorite occupations to visualize and tactualize and otherwise make you the precious sport of my imagination in all sorts of inadequately protected and appointed locations."

"I wish to God you could be here with me. I could do with a bedfellow, want one rather acutely at times. But I confess that what I want just now is

30

you to be in touch with this situation here from day to day, to know the people, to get the intimate sense of the undercurrents, to help me deal with the personal equations.

"These periods of extreme busyness are really the periods when I need you most. Partly of course because I could use you. You could do some things that I have to do and haven't time for, but mainly because things happen that I want to share with you and I simply cannot do it by mail. I want you at my elbow with your wisely curious eyes on all the proceedings. I want you typing in the next room instead of several states away. I have to spatter the drippings of my thought on paper and they reach you two days late. When you read this I may be on a new tack. Come to me. Come as quickly as you decently can. I love you—oh yes—but the point is I need you, my woman, my understander, my discriminating admirer. I want to be admired by a discriminator, I meant a discriminatress, a woman who will admire adequately what I know is admirable, and will reject what I know to be not admirable. You do that pretty well. Sometimes too well for my immediate comfort; more often you lean the other way. But on the whole you do pretty well on that difficult job, and I want you for it."

"Oh yes, it is extraordinary, our history; you at least had something from me entirely unprecedented, something I didn't myself know I had in me. And you handed me something new also, that half yielding—I do not know how to describe it— the barrier that you always kept me conscious of even when you were most at my mercy. I could undress your body almost any time, but the real you would be sure to remain apart, almost disinterested, watching my enterprises, weighing them, calmly critical even while my hands were setting your blood on fire. Rather interesting, what? Well, we have that. Whatever we haven't now or may not have, we can't be deprived of that. It is something to have seized those poignant delights out of this weary saddened world of today, and no one harmed by it, not even ourselves. We can keep those memories without any twinges of conscience."

"Yes, this is a love letter. I feel at liberty to spill this flood of words because I'm your lover, not merely an aspirant, but your lover in fact. I prove it sometimes by invading your body, but I also prove it by invading your mind. I prize your mind, a woman's mind, with that rare and precious supplement, an appreciation, a tolerance of the man's mind. I can walk into your mind at any time and feel at home there. Not because it necessarily agrees with mine, but because it recognizes my mind as being a mind, worthy to cope with it, and sturdily reserves the opinion that it is not unworthy to cope with mine. The usual woman either surrenders intellectually to her husband or remains impressively aloof from his mental operations. You can agree with me intelligently or disagree with me piquantly and without rancor, and it would be hard to say which manifestation is most valuable to me. It is rare either in man or woman, the faculty of disagreeing without rancor, and I prize it accordingly. It is interesting to watch our marriage grow and tie us together, isn't it? Interesting and precious. It makes even separation easier to bear."

I too, with the perversity and uneasiness of ante-marriage all gone out of my relation to him, could

33

live a normal life away from him if I had to, and still be impregnated with him.

"My most intimate friend: I have never had a man for intimate friend before. I like it. I have not exhausted the thrill of it. I like all the things that remind me of it, your common masculine accessories left behind, your socks I make mends in, your pockets that I turn out for the cleaner, the smell of your coat. I am full of memories, not only feel memories but eye and ear memories as well. I suspect I shall always see you in the shaft of light from the wide doorway sitting on the corner of the railing in your good rough clothes, complacently inspecting the stars of heaven while you made leisurely smoke before returning indoors to your wife. Picture of a contented man. No hurry about that man. He has got himself a wife all cooked and waiting to be eaten, and can afford to smoke and inspect the stars. Has got an absorbing job too, and some money here and there, and likes a wife that has the same. The stars are of greater interest under those circumstances, are they not?"

Either is Love

"I have been busy attending to the really important things of life, sorting out and tying up and putting away, and getting out and looking over and doing up, sponging and brushing and cleaning, and in fine inducing my conscience to lie easy and myself to look prosperous when I appear on the pavement in the disguise of your wife. This evening and last evening too, I sat and *sewed*—made a pajama's legs and most of its top, and now pretty soon will have only to put some husband inside of it to have a real bandit all ready to attack me. Speaking of bandits, if you have to get yourself a new hat before I see you, affect one with a wider brim than the last time, something rather fierce in style, to set off the true fierceness of your nature."

"That You in the evening newspaper today was better than most. The one with your hand in your pocket, looking so detached from the proceedings. Ah, you may fool all the people who glance at you there, but you don't fool me. I could just unbutton your waistcoat and walk inside it if I wanted to, and you'd have to do something about it. Ah, God! would you seize me, would you crush me, would

35

you overwhelm me with your mouth and make me limp and melting in your outrageous hands? Wonderful lover that you are—you so sense my needs, you give me so much the very balms my spirit is sick for."

"Oh, I thank Heaven that since I am battered, as you call yourself, you are not less so. That is, I am thankful you do not call upon me for the enthusiasms of my youth, so many kinds and so intense, that have gone into the discard. I do not have to live up to a younger appreciation of life than my own. You rest me.

"Our friend R., for example, has a direct response to mere beauty that you and I haven't so much any longer. And you were asking about P. D. a while ago. Well, P. did revive in me that sensitiveness to beauty to a certain extent while I was accessible to his contagion. But its real life came to an end during my grief over the one person with whom I had lived and loved beauty. We are pretty well suited, you and I, in respect to these things. Neither of us makes the other feel old—or young. P. made me feel intolerably old."

36

Either is Love

"Your visit put new life into me. Today has been exactly one of those winey ones that I longed to share with you. Not a cloud in the sky and the landscape a lawless riot. God, as you say, is a reckless colorist. And now late at night I am alone again by the dying embers downstairs, where you and I have so many times made our poignant excursions into intimacy. This chair, this hearth, and your dinner-coat, its roughness against my breast,—indelible memory. The sweet fierce faintness when you first took down the other shoulder of my chemise—you so silent, so inexpressive, gradually establishing your empire in me, by one means and another tightening the threads that tied me to you. Oh, these conquests of middle-aged reluctant-minded virgins by middle-aged mature intelligent men—there is more real romance in them than all the wooings that sweet young things can ever dream of. I love you as much as anything else for the imprudent unwisdom and sound strategy of your ante-nuptial behavior to me, something that nobody but you, ripe, thoughtful, chaste, demoniacally intelligent, could carry out. I see your face now, in the dim light, curiously afire with purpose of some kind as I have seen it several times, the look of highly civilized man when he perceives his prey, rare enough in your face that shows so little, and prized in my memory accordingly. Your prey! Wonderful that you, governed as you are, worker in the stuff of the mind, with something of the sleepy animal about you, should want your prey like the veriest libertine, and that I should be it! Good God, you leave me no doubts."

"I seem not to have reached the bottom in the long falling that falling in love with you is, but I am powerless to control the progress of it, having once got started. That I should be so subject to a man, the man who seems somehow to have descended into my life as from some airplane out of the sky, without my knowing why, and whose name, curiously enough, people call me by! I am not used to that habit of theirs yet; I notice every time it occurs. And the message that casual use of my married name vaguely carries to me is just that: that desiring you is now my conceded right—that I can make you want me all I wish to, all I am able, if I have the impulse, without doing you any wrong. Of course now that you can have me at your pleasure, my ability to exert any talent for teasing you is much curtailed. But I think maybe I could manage a little of it if we had the leisure and were in the mood."

"I wanted you at that theater last night, and it bothers me to make out why I am so remarkably eager for you to have the fun of seeing other women. I ought to be furiously jealous, but on the contrary, it works quite the other way. There were all the pretty chorus girls, the dancers, the suggestive stage business, the exposé top and bottom—it was good enough of its kind, not coarse but very European— and there was I longing for you beside me to like it and be amused, a pang of wishing for you with every pretty leg that kicked. What *do* we make of that? I'm blessed if I know. But there it is."

Running through the correspondence was the discussion of the "little fat girl" which long remained a measure for us of our safe hold upon one another. He scribbled on club notepaper one noon, "Fashion Notes: 2¾ girls out of every 5 under the age or waist measure of 42½ were wearing some variety.

of the military hat at 12 M. today. The favorite upper garment of ladies including Africans up to 260 pounds has not even vestigial sleeves, and the armhole is increasing in size." He was in a southern city at the time and heat was always a severe strain on him. The fact that women wore so little covering was an exacerbation to his discomfort. He mentioned that a little fat girl stood over his desk and "disturbed the brute" in him in that cloying heat. He did not expect it to worry me, nor did it. On the contrary, there was enhancement in it.

"Ah, beloved, do you think I don't rejoice at the brute in you? I am sorry only for your inconvenience with him in that torrid place. But do you think I want you impervious to the message of the flesh? What right have I to object if you conceivably soil your extraordinary record under the strain? I have always been impatient with wives who leave husbands in the heat of cities while being themselves beyond the reach of discomfort, and have believed they had no right to squeal if things went wrong for them. Though it is not altogether my own doing, in being here I do take advantage of your known habits under these tests. But I feel like crying out to you not to bother about the effect on me. I love you. I sympathize with Mrs. George—do you remember?—who would gladly have fried Hotchkiss in onions for her husband's breakfast. So I say if any little fat girl would make you more comfortable, I would fear injury to her far more than I would fear the infidelity. It wouldn't be infidelity to me— I know that. I would fear a small unpleasant secret kept from me more than anything. Have a little fat girl if it will be the best way for you."

To which he answered:

"No, my dear, the fat girl could not possibly be anything. I like her too well, for one thing. She is a good-natured placid little thing, and I imagine she is one who doesn't know her clothes are indiscreet, which is more than I'd say for most of them. I laugh at your scandalous license to your husband, darling, and yet I suspect you are the woman in a thousand who could not only grant that license but stand by the grant. I believe it strongly enough so that I could undertake to tell you if anything like that should happen. I say could—it would be absurd to promise, for it won't happen."

The fat girl became a symbol:

"I feel I must see you. I feel rather desperate about it. I am not so anxious lest the fat girls get you as I am anxious about your discomforts. But I do also think of that special talent for seduction that you have hidden under a napkin. She who runs may not read it on your outer man, but I hug my knowledge of it and it makes me love you to distraction when it is stirred up, and to want to have it turned upon me."

CHAPTER IV

BEFORE I allowed him to join his life with mine, at the time when he was first becoming so involved with me that it would have done him an irreparable injury to be disappointed in me, I realized over-whelmingly one day that the time had come when he must be told the facts of my previous mating and its dissolution. I was growing so dependent on him that a recoil on his part would cripple me, so whatever the consequences the telling would have to be done before he drew any nearer.

"My affair with you is a pool of crystal clarity," I wrote him, "compared to the turbulent love-stream that is ahead of you in my life. Oh, my dear one, my old grief is upon me at times, excluding you. Even when you are nearest me, it is there. My old memories are tyrannical when I should like best that they be dispelled altogether by my newer ones. Even with all the beauty and treasure of that love that I would not part with, I could wish I had my strongest palpitations and responses to answer you with. You're so charming with your talk of jealousy of the men in my life, so few and so far on its periphery as they have been. They may have sounded many when I gathered up the entire list to review for you at once, but scattered over twenty-five years they are the veriest dodo-birds for scarcity. Were it otherwise I would not be so ingenuously pleased to relate my exploits to you. But if you were to be jealous of the woman in my life, there you would be well within your rights. For there is your rival, the only real one, the only one at all in all my past time. You must have guessed some time ago. I have tried to tell you once or twice,—you have taken from me that there was something, and you must have gathered what it was. Had you shown signs of distaste, you would probably have lost me then and there. Everything now seems to have a bearing on our mutuality. Where I have been living alone for so long, keeping everything to myself, I find myself wanting now to tell every least thing to you. But how to formulate, how to get across to any other mind some most difficult things that are now an integral part of my own? Little by little, perhaps. But even then, never but a little can be told. That love experience was itself a climax, brought about by the many intensities in my varied youth before it. And since it was over, my life is a mere shallow backwater of a life in comparison.

"Even now, some unexpected small thing gives me a moment's overwhelming recollection of the quantity and quality of that absorption; it is such a part of me, never to be changed. It is there, overlaid for long periods, but there, and I despair of ever approaching you to it. When I wrote you that the bare revelation that such a thing had existed was probably an insuperable obstacle to marriage between us, my instinct was perfectly sound. The two things do not accord well; they are inherently at odds. Though you of course in seeming at once to take it so beautifully from me have moved a long step toward their reconciliation. I did not suppose any man could, or would. If only my union with her had not been so peerlessly perfect a union, other loves would consort with it better. One human and flawsome attachment can easily follow another. But how follow a flawsome attachment upon a perfect one? I complain of yours, for example, that it does nothing for my everlasting soul! It doesn't help me toward any great endeavors, as I see—gives no fillip to fine impulses. From you I seem to want your mercy and kindness, and to settle into your security, whereas all the time that she loved me, I was on the stretch to be worthier of it. She was my very soul's complement. Her love held me to my highest possibilities, and even kept raising them to better heights."

"After your wire today that you were coming, my heart pressure went up about ten points, and when I had got in bed, of a sudden—

"Some motor-car vibrating on a rough pavement with fitful lights, and me mercilessly blotted against you in a passion of luscious yielding, while peremptory arm and dominating hand and calculating lips were all at work upon me drawing the soul of me— you little know as yet what you can do with me. Calculating—if I could really teach you that! you have learned so much of how to deal with me—if I could teach you how to reach my lips! So far you

46

are not skilled in that; you have wanted too much too rapidly. You haven't known what is to be gathered on the way. You have tried to reach the full fruit before even the bud was set, if I can say it that way, and my love has felt the shock to its growth. It will take a long time for me to love your lips but you can bring it about if you go slow. Let them propose ideas to my brain but not carry them out, and see the result. Ah, Sweetheart, I am so overflowing tonight. I have seen a girl who reminds me of my old love, and I have been sober and silenced ever since until now. I could do nothing but watch the gait and shoulders and manner that were even so slightly reminiscent to me, and fascinated imagine myself back in the closed marvelous love-life that that was. Kisses! Are you the broad bosom into which I pour all my thoughts, as you say you are? Can I tell you—can I try to put into words for you the miracles she brought to pass to my lips—how heavenly, how diabolically skillful she was? Barely touching the surface she would first let our lips cling just delicately till her message began to flow into me, and even then when my response began she would give no sign but merely cling there. Anticipation would be born in me and mount, and suspense grow and lengthen, and still she would hardly advance. Every moment of inaction became a drama, and then imperceptibly, secretly, one lip would part mine. Gradual was the growth of her mouth's claim upon mine, a long breathlessly attended enactment, heart in heart and at length mouth in mouth, every moment a communion, miracles unfolding between us, in us, carried on through our lips from moment to moment. Afterwards that delight was lost to us through overuse, which is why your kisses are hard for me. The little nerves are temporarily exhausted, hostile to being called on. But you can make your way to them if you are wily and ask very little, make them want just a little more than they get, train them to be dependent on you for nourishment once more. So you can cut off one more retreat for me, retreat into the region where I do not yet love you, one more independence of you. If you could control my mouth as thoroughly as you control me in some other ways, you might have me hand and foot. I long inexpressibly for it, to be owned by and subject to your lips in the same sensitive way as I am at times to your possessing hand."

48

Either is Love

"You know, my dear one, man and woman are not safe together really, until they have got themselves into matrimony, and then perhaps they are too safe for interest. Half the excitement before that is in the mutual sense of insecurity, the fear that they will not come together, and the simultaneous fear that they will come together, prematurely. But woman and woman are safe. We could not mate and no unblest child could rise up to curse us. No avenue leading to malpractice drew us even by a side wind. Ours felt so safe a love! We could let it expand and flower as it would. Though we sank into its arms in total surrender we could not take any harm from it and we could not get into any trouble through it. These many years afterward on some blissful night during one of those flood-tides of believing that you and I were for each other, when I have crept downstairs to you waiting up for me by the fire, it was not safe. Oh no. I wanted then to adventure, to run risks, to test you, to find you out and know you, and you were winning me by loving and enjoying and sparing me. You have been proud to create safety for me with you, and I have adored receiving your ruthlessness and your protection si-

multaneously. It will make me in the end yours.
But as to danger, your nocturnal sessions with me
were all danger, whereas there was not the least
chance or sense of it when she and I were together,
though that togethering had to be even more secretive. The hazard in those years was not that anything could happen to ourselves, but only lest the
ignorant mistaken world should learn, and guess
wrong, and ruin us. I had then something that was
perfection, inspired, Olympian in glory—whatever
extravagant epithet I could devise for it would not
reach up to it—and I concealed it passionately, in a
kind of maternal anxiety to keep it from harm, from
the defilement of false interpretation. I felt it would
have killed me if my love had suffered mishandling
in the minds of others. That was why the precious
gift was always a well-guarded secret, housed only
in the inner shrine of our mutual enclosing solitude.

"You didn't know much what was in my mind
when I was on my way to you in the dark house
those nights when it was you and I who adventured.
You kept putting another log on my fire in the late
night beside your one lamp, without knowing
whether it was going to be worth your while. The

house gave no sign. The reason it gave no sign was because I knew how to turn door-handles upstairs, though a disused room and a back corridor, so that the silence was not stirred, and how to keep the floor and kitchen stairs from giving out that someone was passing over them. It was done by groping in a creeping progress, with long pauses to listen. And I was thinking in exultation as I moved, 'It is a *he* that is there below waiting, a man, made like a man, with a man's thirst and impatience; when he takes me some time, I will know at last the joy of being drained, drawn up, absorbed out of myself, as the sun soaks up water from the earth. It will be final, irremediable, and he will do it. He will bind us. He will know how. I will have no choice. I will at last be so tied that I cannot be lost again. I am going to him now to give him a foretaste, to prevent his ever withdrawing if he would. He will want me so thoroughly after this that he must end by having me.' And then you would see me where I stood in the shadows beyond the doorway.

"I have been used to concealment. The world is so untrustworthy, so stupid in its guesswork. I could never bother with adjusting to the world's misinformation. You see, that other time, the whole business was born, lived its hectic, hindered, abortive life and died its prolonged struggling death, unknown to anyone. Once only I took a trusted friend a little inside the outposts of my confidence. That confidante never betrayed what I wrote her about it, and she is now dead. I wrote her during a time of overflowing happiness, and I never imparted to anyone else the real nature of the friendship that many people superficially saw. I learned thoroughly and over a long time the science of completely covering up the most potent factor operating in my life. Together, no one ever saw us demonstrative. Separated, secrecy was equally unqualified. I learned it so well that now I can't unlearn it easily, even for you.

"I shall, however, try to render some account of it all to you, because it is time and because it is infallibly due you, but I assure you I do not know if I shall be able to go on with it to the end. Telling of it seems like approaching a wave of the sea with a spoon. But I will make an attempt."

CHAPTER V   *To Bart*

WHEN I knew her first she was a spare figure of a girl with very square shoulders slightly advanced above a flat chest, long arms and lean, long, fair, compact hands. Her step was long in proportion to her height, which gave her that salient outdoor elasticity of stride so noticeable inside a room and one of the most characteristic things about her out of doors. She had a small head with a growth of springy gold hair, her only real beauty. Lucky her hair was of that type that always looks well, for she gave it no thought, slapped a brush through it and twisted it up and that was all. If I describe her face I will indicate nothing of what it conveyed to me. It had a regular profile, curves all, and a purity of line especially over chin and throat, that were a delight to the senses. Including its ultramarine eyes it was a round youthful face innocent of its history. I have kissed it so much that its hollows and curves are remembered by my touch better than by my sight. She had slightly spaced teeth, like those of children.

Above all there was her voice. I have always been particularly susceptible to the speaking voice, and delightful voices are many in her part of the country, but hers would have caused the heart to leap in a stone. It was full and mellow, and laughter was always in solution in it. The touch of different speech-accent that belonged with it may have had its share of fascination for me. To hear a word or two of it in the distance when she was arriving back in the evening would make my heart pound for the promise in it. She had a sort of gay, gallant, deferential, highly amused manner. The laughter spattered over in her talk, but it was not the meaningless laughter that is a conversational habit with some people, but a genuine welling up of humor, at herself often, whom she never seemed to take very seriously. She delighted one with her keen relish for other people, and the lively disrespectful way she girded at them. Her rather correct older sisters seemed always to be faintly taken aback by her. Her talk brimmed with vitality and quick wit, fresh as the wind. Her charm, her potent individuality, was

54

an emanation from her mere presence. It was an envelope, an aura, an immanence—I cannot define
anything about it. Yet sometimes I could tire before
she extricated her story from the wealth of incident
she would pile up, and I have more than once pre-
tended sleepiness to call her attention away from
some long narrative to myself.

It was that laughter, suited to the voice-quality
and part of it, the darting fun in her eyes, and the
evidently miscast part she had in the stiff and color-
less party where I met her, that first drew my attention to her. I can see her now—curiously, even very
badly dressed as she was sure to be at that time.
Suitable dress was something that until she had
known me for a time she had never deemed worthy
of a grown person's attention. The strange young
creature was instant in response to this new some-
body, acutely sensitive to the very tame lion of the
evening that was I, and to the interaction set up between me and the group, and gave me all this in a
sentence or two and a gleam of the eye while
swallowing a strawberry out of a punch-glass. My
sudden thought was, "What in the world is this
girl?" I had never seen one like her. I had the im-

pulse to look into her. We talked a little in the hub-
bub.

And then I saw her in a day or two on a horse.
It was, as I realized at sight, seeing that girl where
she lived. We agreed to ride together. And when
we went forth, what riveted my interest upon her,
in addition to her manifest mindfulness of me, was
her remarkable savoir faire of the road and fields, the
beautiful freedom she had on a horse and the effect
she made, quite unaided by any right riding-clothes.
Nobody had good riding-clothes down there—the
better the "family" the more manifest the poverty,
it seemed to me. The Past was the conditioning
fact behind everything that they were, though
they made few references to it. But they did have
some good horses, bred thereabouts, and they
hunted with them as a matter of course, all the
country girls who were good riders joining in. Her
handling of anything whatever under a saddle or in
harness was always to my city-bred eyes a charming
wonder. I discovered that horses behaved as God
meant them to as soon as her soothing hand was on
them. Her hand had always been on them; they
were to her just a phase of her movement, as natural

and personal as walking. As for me, she let out her laughter, her welling free laughter without a hint of rudeness in it, again and again that first day, at my conscious deferential treatment of my borrowed horse, and my interest in and concern for him. I knew something of the current patter about horses and hunting, and something of the behavior that goes with them, but she knew what to *do*.

As I write it recollections throng. In her own country, child of her upbringing that she was, this was not strange. But the horse was her familiar anywhere. The episode at the Roman Hunt is still remembered by the friends we were with. We had been invited to drive out to the meet with some English people in Rome, and were standing in a little group among some hundred others near the starting-point, when suddenly a riderless horse came thundering amok, stirrups beating, head high in outrage at whatever it was that had happened, charging every way in his flight. The visitors of course scattered like leaves. One or two women fell, trying to run. All save the one American girl. In one of the moments when he was checking and swerving, searching a clear way through, she made a sharp leap at the bridle and hung on while dragged some little distance by the momentum. But when the excited grooms and spectators closed in, the horse though trembling was being soothed neck and head by practiced hands, and when she turned him over to them and came back to us beating at the dust in her skirts, she was laughing at the agitation.

Besides riding once or twice after our first encounter, she managed to carry me off to drive alone, ostensibly to give a visitor some view of the surrounding country. We drove out of the road across fields, and there, as I took a large watch out of her belt to see if we must turn back, she kissed me. I was completely taken aback, distinctly uncomfortable, certainly devoid of pleasure. I had never been demonstrative with my friends, and I had very understanding and deep-reaching friendships. I thought this was a beginning friendship like another, though it seemed a very charming and soon indeed a very obsessing one. Another day she sat with her back to a tree and looked at me, her hands limp beside her, and I was suddenly moved to trace the outline of her face and said, "Can it be real that I am here so near you?" for we had already begun to feel the check that seemed to operate whenever we tried to meet. But if she made to catch me to her impulsively, I wouldn't have it. That direction for our affection seemed fraught with danger to me. I had repulsive memories of over-affectionate pairs of girls in college.

I remembered clearly for some years the sequence of the early developments, but when the tragic end came and merely to recall was to agonize, I washed most of the events out of my mind. If I still had the correspondence I could reconstruct all the first steps, but if I still had the correspondence I would never write a line of this. Merely to read in it would crumble my long-built-up peace. After the débâcle I put all my great bundles of letters into the furnace in a single gesture of execution, and exacted the same from her. It had to be done. We had written as fully and as freely as we talked. Any other eye falling upon and misconstruing what had been for us alone might have involved us in wrong that nothing could have righted, and at that time no sympathetic interpretation seemed ever likely to be possible.

Why was no sympathetic interpretation possible?

Well, you know that after all psychology is a very recent science. We have lately been so steeped in its fast-thickening brew that we forget how elementary the study was a short while ago. At that time no one had ever yet said sublimation. James' textbook was practically the only one in this country written for the grasp of the ordinarily educated. And how small was James' field compared to the scope of psychology today! Stanley Hall had written his pioneer book on adolescence, but it stood alone and the layman would hardly be inclined to read it. Havelock Ellis, the Michelangelo of sex psychology, was only beginning to build; his masters Kraft-Ebing and the earlier Europeans were nearly unknown over here. Even the moderate-voiced Ellen Key, even Olive Schreiner, were only for the very emancipated. Though some understanding of a case such as ours would exist now in the high places of psychology, nothing about unusual manifestations of sex was accessible in those years when I was so smitten and so helplessly ignorant. There were no bureaus, no research societies, no bibliographies in our subject. Against a question such as ours the world we knew would have closed a chilly door and refused to recognize or listen. Had it surmised the state of affairs no matter how innocent, we would have been suspected of something nameless and iniquitous. I myself had harshly judged one or two instances of too close alliance between girls of my acquaintance. We had no course but to destroy the evidence, and continue to preserve the secrecy.

CHAPTER VI   *To Bart*

I HAVE often wondered what part the opposition that my friendship with Rachel encountered played in its rapid blossoming. Finding ourselves hindered by other people was enough to give considerable added intensity to our sensation of each other. I did not at all understand why so much management seemed to be required merely for her to come to tea with me, why that simple friendliness had to be wrapped in discretion and diplomacy. One day when she was coming to see me and did not, I received a letter from her. It was the first in that incandescent sequence that afterward became life itself for me. It presented me her characteristic angular scrawl at its very best, more like a respectable penmanship than any I ever saw again from her. She must have taken immense pains with it. She said she was writing in a little cove by the river, with Brummel tethered to a tree. In it she tried to tell me what was on her mind.

Either is Love

But how little I took in of her meaning! Something of her strange previous history she hinted at, her fear of herself, her fear of hurting others, and that she was tied in other ways than in her home and at her work. She was nevertheless passionately attracted to me and seemed to want to warn me that it probably meant trouble. "Now that I have a pass to your sensibilities," she said, she perceived the cold draughts that lay waiting outside the enclosing warmth of our young interest in one another. She took alarm for me. But I couldn't take it for myself. I saw no reason why the trouble need amount to much. The warning meant nothing to me.

Having to snatch half-hours from hostile conditions in order to talk was not calculated to allay our early excitement. The result was usually that we spent the short time mostly in looking at each other. From the first we had always to meet watch in hand. All our interchange had in it that heart-tightening consciousness of imminent separation. Not until she came to me in Europe two years later did we ever have release from that constant check to our joy— the immediate prospect of losing it again.

But we could write letters. We initiated that

voluminous record of our love, threshing out every aspect of it, on which for long periods later we subsisted altogether. The first tentative self-conscious exchanges gradually became long delights of revelation. When I had to go away for a time, I soon lived for nothing else. I sat in the garden of my hotel with my writing-block, weaving the distant hills into dreams, and destiny seemed focused in the moment of the arrival of the mail. Under the compulsion to make ourselves known, we were recounting all of ourselves to each other in those first letters, our presents and our pasts, our anticipations and our problems.

But chiefly we were trying to understand where we were. We had met briefly six or eight times only, mostly in the presence of others, over a period of a few weeks, but we were unmistakably, deeply in love, and knew it. It was the first time for me, though not, as she soon told me, for her. But for her this experience was entirely over and beyond anything she had known before. She was incredulous at her own capacity for more love, and her state of rapture was qualified with that fear lest she be bringing me some eventual hurt or suffering. I saw

no reason for any suffering, but there were those evident and unexplained barriers that I was begging to
be allowed to understand, and did not. That first
separation was the happiest of the many that we endured, for it had in it only our immense preoccupa-
tion with each other, and the counting away of the
slow but definite weeks before we meant to come
together. She grew in me every day with an almost
immoderate growth. Our letters were always unfinished business. The ball bounded back almost
before it touched, and every topic multiplied itself
into a dozen more.

In those letters we gradually worked out a scheme
whereby we could secure privacy together for some
approaching months. She uncovered for us a somewhat dilapidated old place in the country that she
would be able to reach after work from Washington.
All I had to have for my own work then beginning
was a writing-table, which I could have on a rather
rickety brick porch with iron railings. We could be
assured of something probably more or less casual in
the nature of meals provided by a colored woman
who was the mother of nine, along with a choice of
somewhat arklike rooms. And we would be able to

devote evenings and Sundays to our prime business which was to become acquainted as well as to be in love.

When the moment at last actually came, and I was tearing through space to her by train, I folded my writing-block in the prospect of having my incredible new love at face-to-face distance only. Yet when I was met at the railroad station by a nearly strange young woman, I remember thinking as I followed her from the platform, "How can I suppose I love her? I have never seen her but a few times. She is practically unknown to me."

That first living arrangement that we achieved in our dilapidated house was, until the bombshell shattered it, our incredible honeymoon, as we loved calling it. It was all the heaven that any honeymoon could be, the first delicate and fearful approach of two highly organized souls in the silence of their own heartbeats, .and the gradual, still, heartbreakingly beautiful absorption of one within the other. "If we had to give this up now," I remember saying to her early in that time, "I should be ten years in getting over it."

Step by step we let the slow union take place, not

without misgivings and pauses for breath and orientation, for, overwhelmingly in love though I was, or perhaps because of it, I was passionately on the alert for the least spot, the least mote of suspicion by my own sense of integrity. The unheard-of nature of this thing, the lack of precedent, confused and worried me, and my intelligence had one eye sleeplessly open surveying the tendencies of my heart. The first time that she said, in the dusk of the garden after a long silence with my hand resting on her throat, "Do you belong to me?" I recall violently whispering, "No! No! I belong to myself." And I leaped up and left her and dealt with my emotions under the stars, while the bunched heap on the ground never stirred a muscle. Terrifyingly sweet as it was, touch disconcerted me for a long time. I was in terror of liking her for any tendency to mastership that might be in her. The possibility of the false male was a thing I was in arms against.

Her vocation of chemistry has since attracted thousands of women, but at that time there were very few women working in any of the sciences. In her world until the Great War came these things were nothing that a "lady" could by rights do. But

67

the scientific training had come easily to her, and she could laugh her way over opposition and into her loved laboratory without outraging somehow the susceptibilities of the community, where another would have raised a storm. I think her people were probably vague as to what it was that was done in a laboratory anyway. She was up there away from them in the city and when she came home she was the same girl that she had been before. I saw, however, an element in her personality of pioneering, of resistance already overcome, of carelessness of opinion and of Goal ahead, that carries a definite masculine connotation rather than feminine. But watching her, it was a slow relief to me to find that in general it was the little masculine touches in her that I liked least, not most.

She was pathetically grateful to me in her turn for cultivating the feminine in her. All her earlier friends had liked and encouraged her boyishness, and she responded to my different attitude about that with immense charm. Her boyishness had but little attraction for me and to encourage it seemed to me to do her an injury. Its presence between herself and me would have contaminated everything.

68

Either is Love

My lover was a girl, a particularly attractive girl, with initiative and strength of personality above most, to be sure, but a girl with all the primary feminine capacities. How I glowed over helping her form her own ideas of dressing herself. What tender joy we had over her first charming and appropriate dress bought abroad two years later, with the graceful lines properly draping her young figure. We had her lively hair arranged for some cleverly made hats, and I adored the results of my work. She liked it too, and would practice her young arts of bewitching upon me with deliberate deviltry, to my intense delight. The one of us lived vicariously in the other, and though a sensual quality was a large part of our pleasure in each other, the fact is that it was sensuality between loving young women, and not of a loving young woman for the other gender in disguise. In this was the very soul of the phenomenon. If it was she who wooed, that was because being more experienced she wanted to go faster than I, and so at first took more of the initiative. It was I on the other hand who was the more imaginative; later on it was I who devised most of the ways we found of manifesting our love. She was my woman-mate, never a pseudo man-mate. If she took a sensuous pleasure in my body, it was mainly through her sense of beauty to which it happened to cater, since illness had not yet taken the youth and correctness from its lines. Though I had not till then thought of there being anything about me to satisfy a lover, I began to play at being beautiful for her eyes. We saw a reproduction of a Swedish marble that symbolized us, and that we took for our own. It was a seated austere nude with another young figure prostrated before it, the forehead just touching the knees. The best of young love was in it.

Her beauty for me lay mostly in the exquisite spacing of her profile which I could never worship enough, that curve of chin so young and innocent-looking and alluring, and in her square determined shoulders and long fair sensitive hands. She wasn't so exceptional otherwise, in spite of her marine eyes, though I loved all of her and did homage to her. She was moreover extraordinarily susceptible through her finger-tips, which I am not. The skill, the power, the high art she had in her hand to convey messages from her brain to mine—no words could set it down. It made her my owner while her touch was upon me—it transformed me. That reverential sense for beauty and joy that came into me from her hands is something I can never know a second time. She took me with it.

After becoming acquainted with kisses I remember imposing a whole week of abstinence upon us until I should have time to take account of myself and determine what to do. I do not regret one moment of fulfillment lost through conscientiousness. Our love was nurtured in it; moral integrity was half its life to us. Indeed I knew fiercely that I could not enjoy at the expense of my instinctive feeling of what was all right.

I used to leave my brick portico when it came time for her to come home, and make my way down through the tangle of old yews and laurel in what had once been a garden, to where some iron seats were hidden. Then when she swung in through the distant gate and turned her long unhasting step to where she knew she would find me, we were at last alone and could exchange the longed-for food for eyes and hands. Talk came first, what Mr. G. had thought, how Miss M. was working out, how the current experiment seemed to be tending and what had to be done next, all the interests that had been in her day. Her short tired evenings, a total of two or three hours, we spent in acquainting each other with all our concerns, always canvassing the possibilities for the whole of life together. We delighted to find we had the same taste in poetry. The old lilacs surrounding the iron seats heard much poetry read aloud. Good poetry was in those years a necessity to me, but that requirement more or less died with her passing from me.

Then, late one night, she begged me, "Let me stay! This once, let me stay!" I hadn't thought of that—it was a total surprise to me. But, why not? It wasn't as if she were a man, or anything like a man. Why should my bed be denied to this girl who had my heart? So in the end I looked once more at her face on the pillow before putting out the light. I needn't tell you what the first unhindered embrace is, every muscle contributing. I thought my initiation that night complete, that no more was possible to me. In the morning I felt my face must have altered; hers had—it had new eyes.

To succeed somehow in making a coalition out of us was the pressing urgency in both of us. Since

72

there was no usual route to union that we could follow, we had to fall back on symbols, fondnesses that could be figuratively interpreted, through representation, through the messages of physical metaphor—if I make myself understood. I recall how once we were in an open-air seat somewhere where there was a crowd; it was cold and we had a rug with us. We wrapped the rug about us. In doing so our hands met accidentally under it, my right hand and her left. A fuse lit. I left my hand open on my knee expectant. Slowly her fingers began to explore my palm. With exquisite delay one by one a finger stretched along and lay flat against my corresponding finger, and ultimately, by degrees, her thumb completed the circuit upon my thumb, and her palm laid itself down upon mine. Hand to hand, all the hand knowing all the hand, a current coursing around the nerve-circle, it was as if we lay quiveringly heart to heart, warmly one, secretly sensual, in the cold of outdoors and the crowd of people. It was all the satisfaction we needed; it absorbed us, it fulfilled us for the time.

It was a gratifying thing to me that I was slightly the taller—that helped to dispel the possibility of any pseudo-masculine nonsense which her disregard of clothes and feminine interests, her free walk, her chemistry, her "horsiness," could easily suggest, and which I detested. I had not often been thought tall. And to find she fitted into me so charmingly, her shoulder just under mine, her head where it could rest under my neck, so that we could stand or lie comfortably curved into one another like a pair of teaspoons was itself a joy, for the meaning it carried. I depended on her, but she too depended on me. Each held the other in her bosom, in solution, in mutual completion.

The same meaning was in her hand, her charged hand that was capable of lighting a flame wherever it came to rest. The field of secondary sex-responses is overlooked by man and woman, eagerly pushing on toward something final. The talent in her hand was creative of unlimited beauty. Wherever it chanced to establish a meeting-place for us, there I rushed and lived, moment by moment thirstily receiving her message and giving back my own for her to read. I was only less sensitized to her mouth than to her hand, but in either was a refinement in the technique of communication only to be experienced when mouth and hand were all there were, not prelude only. In this realm of symbolism we were prodigal of invention. The wonder of her weight upon me was something only translatable in terms of the mind. When she came to wake me before leaving in the early morning all hatted and fresh, she made a swift ritual of farewell to my breast, a sensitive joy that I could hold, under the warm covers, for an hour or two longer. And yet she might not pretend to the rights either of a man or of a child. As my woman-mate she could take all that crossed neither of the other anticipations. Sensuous delight certainly—volupté of a particularly exquisite kind. But nothing fraudulent, no forgery of another signature. In these distinctions we were sound, and we were unwavering, because they were instinctive.

CHAPTER VII

IT took me a long time to be able to put this all to paper for the friend to whom I was committing myself. I could do it only by degrees, a little at a time. I sent it to him in installments, and it was only the constant encouragement I had from him that enabled me to go on.

"I seem not to be jealous," he was writing, so remarkably, "of that earlier love of yours. Why it should be I do not know, but so it is. As I get more and more in touch with the affair, I find not jealousy but an increase of tenderness for you, widowed, the more like me for that, the more understanding, better understood. I am passionately eager to know about it. To know all about it. Will you ever be able to tell me all, dear heart?

"Who was she? What was she? What exactly and in the greatest and most intimate detail, did she do in your life? What was it that came between you at the end? It may be hard for you, perhaps painful, to satisfy a curiosity so exigent. If you were lying on my breast on a quiet night before the library fire, I think I could draw that knowledge from you without hurting you. To get it on paper for me is different. Do you remember, best beloved, just barely hinting to me of this affair, and asserting in the next breath that the mere fact of your having done so was an insuperable obstacle to our marriage? I didn't argue with you, but I said then in my heart that your halting, partial revelation was the longest step you had yet taken in my direction.

"I had no sooner had hands on you than I knew that I was dealing with a woman of experience. How to account for that experience, how to reconcile it with what I knew of your history, with your expressed opinions, was a problem of some proportions; I can tell you it was comfortable to lean on my knowledge of the staunch clear-sighted clean-minded comrade of that first winter, in the assurance that whatever the solution might be, it couldn't possibly touch your essential integrity.

"I hesitated to ask you for the story," he said,

"not merely because I wanted to spare you but because I was a little doubtful of what it might do to me. But I felt it was necessary to take the chance. If I couldn't stand your previous history there was a bad obstacle to the growth of our relation. But now it is these confessions of yours that have confirmed my possession of you, because you have been giving me this secret chapter in your life, because you have licensed me to probe further into it. Your letters stir me always, your progression towards me, your shrinking from me, oh any of the moods that your letters reflect, but I can take them in at one sitting and go back to my job. This supreme experience of yours, and your turning it over to me so unreservedly, so wonderfully, the beauty and the suffering, is more moving than all. It stirs me profoundly. I've still some reserves about this Rachel. You have me—well, you have me a damned sight more completely than I thought any woman could ever have me—even when I began to think of marrying you. But you haven't me to the extent of making my intelligence accept Rachel—not yet. I wait for the catastrophe. All that you have told me, what you will tell me when I have you in my arms and question you, I can take. Yet why in the name of God did that relation come to nothing? I can with difficulty wait for the answer. When you tell me, my darling, of the wonder of the weight of her body on yours, I feel no grudge against her, only an immense and rather intolerable longing. Competing with a woman for the love of a woman is something that my sophisticated intelligence can fully present to itself, but the notion does not strike home into that primeval realm where jealousy is chiefly bred. That love affair lacked a man. The truth is I love you. I merely love you more, the more you tell me about Rachel."

CHAPTER VIII

To Bart

DURING that month when Rachel and I were root-
ing ourselves in the sweet fragrant soil of our new
emotional country, we were not without increasing
consciousness of storm-clouds. The obstructions
familiar to lovers—other ties, distance apart, exacting
work, insufficient money—we of course had those;
they are problems out of which the usual lovers can
usually hope to find a way. If they have engaged
themselves they will be expected to come together
and will probably be helped to do it. But woman and
woman have no prescriptive right to each other; any
number of other obligations are thought by all their
world to come first. In our case the ordinary ob-
stacles were formidable enough, but there were two
others of an even more serious character.

There was the mother, my Rachel's mother, to
whom as youngest child she was always loyally
tender—Rachel's mother unalterably opposed the

new friendship from the beginning, and refused point-blank even so much as to make my acquaintance. Of course I was a Yankee and they would be a little suspicious of that, but it would by no means keep me out of their home. I had not been allowed to have the faintest guess at the real opposition, which Rachel was hoping and expecting to overcome before I need know of its existence. But as early as I first began to reach out to her, I perceived that about her life there were obscure bonds and meshes. I on my side was all romantic impatience to come into the circle of her hearth, to ask affection of her family. I wanted the new alliance recognized by the world with happiness and celebration. Or failing that, I would have been grateful for the opportunity to put our dilemma before someone older in wisdom and have it given careful and sensible thought for us. But most often when I made my eager gestures toward Rachel's people they were gently deflected through one excuse or another. Our early encounters alone, always so strangely brief, had taken much planning and counter-planning, and usually for four or five arrangements made only one would survive, without any very clear explanation of what was hindering them. It was only long afterward that I learned the reason through Rachel's confessions.

And the second and most serious obstruction was Elaine.

Elaine was a slightly older woman who at first seemed to be merely often about. For some time I hardly took in her importance. I saw an aquiline person with much dark hair and an imperturbable habit of conversation, but so occupied as I was in the delicate business of securing a relationship with Rachel, I was only partially aware of the talkative cousin, as one among the many hampering presences. Even when I realized that she had some kind of permanent place in Rachel's family, different from that of the large loose group of relatives coming and going, I did not appreciate the bearing of that upon our affairs.

What I learned in the course of time from Rachel herself was that while the love of woman was of baffling newness to me, it was not quite so new to her. Her family had had to witness and see her through some painful manifestations of it. She had had, ever since she first defied her traditions and got away to college, a succession of adventures of the heart with other girls. Her role in these youthful devotions had been chiefly quixotic. She had been of use to all the friends in one way or another—helping them out of scrapes, abetting their love affairs, securing audience for their talents. I could not see that they had ever done anything in return. There had finally been an affair centering about a rather lurid young creature with stage propensities whom the gallant Rachel believed she could "save." Her infatuation for this Jenny, the terrific scenes that Jenny made and the abnormal psychology she spattered about, created a great commotion among the family and nearly drove the mother to distraction. It was no doubt a poor business. When young Rachel came to the realization that she was being basely used and that Jenny could never be anything but a parasite, there was a violent concussion and a recoil. An asylum was ready in the shape of the faithful cousin, and all the worried train of stepbrothers and aunts and married sisters who had been so uneasy without knowing exactly what about, were relieved when Elaine had received the prodigal to her unromantic bosom, found a position for her in Washington not unrelated to her own, and

took over the supervision of their common life. The
prodigal, though shaken, was objective by nature.
She betrayed no bitterness; she believed she was
done with passion, and she fitted into her job with
surprising success. Elaine watched over her, managed their mutual affairs and invested their savings,
and made those clothes which they seemed to wear
at times interchangeably. Into the deeps of Rachel's
life Elaine never really reached, but to Rachel that
was as well—she imagined the deeps closed over forevermore. And for some years she had been jogging
along in this one-sided double harness when she met
me.

But what strangely occurred—what baleful accident—was that I, all innocent of any of this history
and some years after it, arriving as from a different
planet into Rachel's home country, I had the misfortune to resemble in outer woman the girl Jenny,
the ancient enemy. When I came upon the scene
and Rachel manifested interest in me, it struck terror
to all their hearts. It was no wonder they were
hostile—they saw nothing in me but a revival of
their early anxieties. To Rachel the resemblance was
the most amusing of coincidences. She never tired

of her astonishment that two people at opposite poles in type, in mind, in behavior, in background and in personal history, even in race, should look so much alike as myself and the Jenny of turbulent memory. But to Rachel's mother and to Elaine, neither of whom allowed themselves to know me, the mere sight of me was enough to set their nerves on edge. Rachel knew better than to expose me to sure rebuff. She meant to win her mother's hospitality for me before I should encounter her at close quarters. But traditional as hospitality was in that family, inalienable, almost, to their code, Rachel never reached the point where she dared try to bring me within its reach.

Three long years afterward, when Rachel was with me in Europe, I received from the mother who had for those three years been so consistently my enemy, a touching recantation. It was the first communication of any sort that I had ever had from her, and it was a letter written in regret for her misunderstanding of me, even asking forgiveness as if that were necessary, and expressing gratitude for what she was pleased to consider I had done for her daughter. But this was after she had bitterly thwarted

Either is Love

Rachel's whole connection with me for the entire three years that we had been trying to establish it, when in our bewilderment and pain and separation any kindness would have been precious, any confidence a support.

Now Elaine, in her fear that I represented a recurrence of the dangerous for Rachel, was engaged throughout that month of our first happiness together in thick daily letters of remonstrance and discussion as to Rachel's "right" to love anyone else at all. Elaine took the ground, earnestly and tenaciously, that in accepting her own complete devotion Rachel had assumed the responsibility toward her of undivided allegiance. Elaine argued that the unstable history of Rachel's affections made it a matter of moral integrity not to engage in any more affairs of the heart—a conviction that was convenient in the circumstances. In trying to keep me out of Rachel's life she maintained that she was not actuated in the least by jealousy. This seemed to Rachel and me to be mere rationalizing; of course Elaine was jealous—she had every right to be. I recognized and have always known that their relation had no element of passion in it, but jealous of Elaine I on my side most

86

decidedly was. Of course. She wanted to pre-empt the person I adored. My belief is that a certain amount of jealousy is inherent in any thorough love; it need not be given rein or allowed to become a spring of thought or action, but not to acknowledge it is not to be frank. I considered my jealousy of Elaine as an increased call to protect her interests, but Elaine was sure that there was no jealousy at all in her affection for Rachel. She was standing for principle only. Rachel, so far from agreeing that she was lost to honor if she allowed her interest in me to take root, was convinced in the glow of her young fervor that all her hopes for higher development lay within it. Elaine held that by all the canons of constancy and wisdom she should be first in Rachel's life; Rachel insisted that no question of first or second existed, that she cared for different people differently, and might care for as many as she pleased. She certainly intended to cleave to Elaine and not cause any sorrow to anybody, but she meant to make room, in a quite different compartment of her life, for me. Loyalty was one of the primary springs of her nature and she would never have wittingly shaken off any faithful friend.

I for my part believed that such a merger as Elaine had formed of their joint living was against the real interests of both of them. As I became aware of their informal habits and careless mutual ownerships and usages—books, towels, beds, pocket-books, hats and friends—I found myself disdainful. As soon as she perceived that Elaine's liking and appreciation of me were not to be a matter of course, Rachel's eyes were opened to the folly of having allowed her identity to be so swamped. The truth was that at the time that Elaine had taken over the management of their joint existence, Rachel was too heartsick and disillusioned to care what happened, probably even welcomed the freedom from decision. But indeed as I revert to it now, what is the distinction between a merging of stockings and finances on the one hand, and on the other a merging of the whole heart and soul, such as we were engaged in, though carefully preserving the proper division of clothing and checkbooks? I still think that if I had been allowed a knowledge of their mutual situation in the beginning, what followed could all have been different. I had access to Elaine at first, could have demonstrated my sincerity as to Rachel's welfare and my extreme unwillingness to injure herself. But I knew of no claims to Rachel on this Elaine's part or anybody's, or any reason for explaining myself to an indefinite cousin in the house, and after it became evident to Elaine that Rachel had more than a pleasant friendly feeling for me, she passionately put up the barriers between us, recognized no rights whatever on my part and refused to permit me to join the discussion in any way.

Elaine, further, couldn't be treated in cold blood, for she was the victim of a recurring nervous illness against which she always made a courageous fight. Rachel's role in this illness had been at times no less than that of preserver. Her remarkably efficient handling of the case in emergencies had made her nearness to the patient something that neither of them could well avoid. She had had no wish to avoid it till now, and never at any time sought release from the obligation to the cousin, even when she was sorely taxed on account of it. She had of course a real affection in that quarter, and there was a strong expiatory vein in Rachel which gave rise to eternally recurring generosities of conduct.

When I first came down into the county and met

Either is Love

Rachel there on her holiday, things had been going pretty well for some time past, it seemed. She was devoted to the fast-developing work she was connected with, and was making herself of pronounced value in it. Elaine had her own by no means negligible position, and they were not at the time in joint living quarters though that had been customary. But it appeared now that anxiety over the newly introduced serpent in the Eden, and the arguments they were having over Rachel's unwillingness to expel me promptly from her life, were occasioning fresh manifestations of the depression that might so easily bring on the trouble again. I was allowed to make no presentation of our case as it seemed to me to affect us all, because of Rachel's fear of the results of the excitement for Elaine. And the matter was strictly between themselves, stated the patient; I had no right even to know that she was suffering because of me. So Rachel, expecting always to dissolve the opposition by reason, kept me long in ignorance of what I was causing. When I did learn I was by then in the grip of the biggest emotion of my life, and longed for Rachel as the saints crave for God.

CHAPTER IX   *To Bart*

WHEN Rachel asserted her independence and made the arrangement for living with me for a season outside the city, she believed that Elaine would yield to accomplished fact and would in time be persuaded of its harmlessness. But one evening when my lover came home more tired than usual, I soon saw that she was hiding something from me. She could not tell me what had happened. But our tender seclusion that was meaning so much to us was doomed. Elaine's situation had suddenly required that she repossess her nurse. It was an emergency in which Rachel could see no choice. Even though it might be the result of Elaine's unrecognized desire to separate us at whatever cost to herself, illness was illness and had to be reckoned with. There was no one but Rachel who could serve.

It was no wonder she could hardly tell me. This was not only the knell of our immediate prospects—

it was far more than that. We needed outrageously, in the grip of our young passion, to calm some of the drive of it by contact. We had neither guide nor precedent for conduct in such a case. Neither ·she nor I had ever known, either in life or in literature, any two who were similarly affected. Her previous devotions had nothing of the quality of this one— they gave her no illumination at all regarding what had now befallen her. In my combined agony and beatitude I was in a state of mental and emotional ferment that was beyond anything I had ever myself known of as between man and woman. Unless we could be given time to find our feet together and work our way out slowly and carefully to firm ground, the situation held actual dangers for us. With a few months ahead of us we might hope to succeed in bringing some order into our problem and some abatement into our excitement—we were entirely bent on doing so. Now we were frustrated before we had really begun. The antagonist of our happiness joined us in our retreat.

My first instinct of course was flight. Elaine did not like me—if some condition of her own obliged her to invade the solitude in which we were grappling with our stupendous new force, it was only decent of me in the face of it to take the spectacle of myself out of the way while she was there. I began at once to pack. But Elaine had apparently no mind to let that happen. When Rachel mentioned it, I learned that to drive me away would cause her cousin the most acute distress. She must obviously not be more distressed; distress was the worst thing for her. Surely we could behave with reasonable courtesy for a while without any reference to our difficulties. Surely we could. The imperturbable habit of conversation took care of that. It took possession of our evening meals, Elaine's bright competent monologue addressing itself to Rachel, politely including me on the distant horizon of her civility. During the day in Rachel's absence the other two of us kept out of each other's way. To me it was absurdly humiliating to be debarred from the one topic that pressed for explanation and settlement, but she took the convenient attitude that I did not exist for her. As soon as she was established in the double room with Rachel, she resumed all her usual direction of their joint affairs, precluding participation by the mere acquaintance who happened to be under the same roof. It shames me to recall my exasperation over her small insults, perfectly unintentional as they were because she took no trouble to imagine into my case. I had assuaged my abject craving to be useful to my love, to work in some way for her, by mending and cleaning for her, by a multitude of small observances such as one woman can have for another. Elaine knocked at my room to relieve me of the stocking-basket and any of Rachel's strayed possessions, closed all doors upon me, and continued to insist I should not go away.

I cannot revert to that period even now without a feeling of physical weakness. Indeed I stripped all of it from memory afterwards as well as I could. I held myself in a vise of will day after day, night after night. Need of my dear one clawed at me; our affairs were demanding with extreme urgency some far-sighted thinking out together, but mere meetings were frustrated by the nature of the situation in the further room. It was sickening to remain there, but as often as I started to go, I was stopped again by word of the seriously agitating effect the news had upon the invalid. Consideration of her plight had always to take precedence of ours. But remaining, I might not share any of Rachel's brief transits. If she stayed away from their room more than a few minutes at a time, upon her return the patient would be in a threatening condition. I lived the miserable days through, however, solely for that possible short hour of evening, but when it came, the specter of the white face beyond a few partitions was between us and kept us apart. She will never know the brakes we put upon ourselves out of compassion for her. Our harried search for a way out of the dilemma went round and round in a circle. Elaine must not be left alone for long. Elaine was ill, whether mentally or physically did not alter the situation; she was easily made worse and already cruelly hurt and very brave. Our short renewal of confidence and love, though taken only through the eyes, was all that Rachel had to keep her going throughout her own ordeal. Indeed if I were to leave we would both be abandoning our only fount of strength. Yet staying seemed to be slowly finishing me.

I witnessed one of the crises, and it was sobering. I was summoned in the night. The patient was unconscious and apparently in the death throes. Rachel was officiating skillfully with things out of bottles when I reached the bedside. She directed me where and how to massage. We both worked swiftly and in silence. When consciousness began to return she sent me out so that I should not be recognized. I sat on the staircase on call for an hour or so, staring at the wall in dismay at the sounds from inside—"Oh, let me go, let me go!" (always the first cry on regaining consciousness, I knew) in a reiterated moan, the long silences followed by small abrupt movements, the patient's weakened gutturals, the low reassurances and business-like commands of Rachel. When Elaine appeared next day she behaved to me as usual, pleasantly civil as to a casual acquaintance, unconsciously displaying her proprietary intimacies and prior rights to Rachel. The things I took from that sick woman, who would not open her rancor to me, which I might have abated! There was a famous doctor whom she was willing to be taken to, and she set date after date for their departure to New York to see him, only to be obliged to postpone again. At length after weeks of the ordeal and still no end in sight, Rachel and I allowed ourselves one single draught of each other a day. Returning at night, she stopped in my quarters long enough to drain off through our lips some small part of our dammed-up passion, without any words whatever, because of Elaine waiting in anguish, but still some release against the stricture of the next twenty-four hours. Though three people underwent nearly a maximum of suffering during that time—or perhaps there is no maximum to suffering—Rachel at least, as she often assured me, had positively not time to suffer as either of us waiting for her did. She had the asylum of her active day's work, and well might that have suffered, had Rachel been anyone else. But Rachel never disintegrated. She throve on responsibility, and if she did less than her customary distinguished work in spite of the strain in her private life, I did not know it.

There is something irreducible in all this. We were in a trap from which, struggle as we would, we could find no escape. To me it was a situation wholly without precedent—no code I knew of covered it. Unmarried young women were not supposed, were not known, to have attachments of any such tenacious and formidable a character. What so tragic for a person of Rachel's undoubted place in the world to have one more or one less friendship out of her wide acquaintance? Who had ever heard of friendships making any such demands as were being made upon Rachel by not only one person but two? Connections between women still receive commonly an amused tolerance when it is not a more or less expressed reprobation. That a passionate affiliation of two persons of the same sex may be not only decent but morally constructive was being evidenced to me by daily experience. Yet such a quasi-marriage between responsible women, what help may it claim from society? We asked ourselves that; there was no answer. I looked about in vain for some living person known to me whom I could trust or could ask to advise me. The fear, since a problem like ours had no recognition in any literature or morals that we knew, that there must be something degenerate about us, disturbed me not a little, yet I could only admit that we were not degenerate. We were both of us, all three of us, in fact, in that class of young American professional women who do much of the leading, the building, the studying and organizing in our times, and are accustomed to giving little or no heed to the call of self-gratification.

Either is Love

We were an anomaly, and I could not explain us; but if we were unique—and even now I wonder if we were not something like unique—I knew that Rachel and I were fundamentally sound, at bottom I knew it with all my instincts and all my intuitions.

The last stage of the inquisition was after their departure, that month that I passed in suspense before Rachel could return to me alone and the blessed sun shone out again for a time upon our love. That span of desolation is like a nightmare where it survives in my recollection. No other passage in all my varied life has ever equaled it in intensity of misery. Probably the later separations which were longer and had less hope in them became more of a condition of living, like the walls of a penitentiary. But in that first sentence I served, every moment that had to be endured as it came was like a fresh cruelty of flouted longing. I cannot hear the shrill sweet cry of the cardinal-bird today without a turning-over sensation below the diaphragm, or smell the honeylocust. The red berries of the pipsissewa have the same effect—we had made them so personal to us— I can never divorce that plant from the feeling of purgatory. A few brain-pictures remain to me—myself in a grove of trees where I used to go to allay a little the ache in my arms by surrounding a tree with all my physical strength, like a drunkard around a lamp-post. Myself hanging over the oil-heater in my draughty room, drinking the malted milk which was nearly all I lived on, a ray of comfort penetrating to my ache in the fact that the clock had moved on fifteen minutes since the last time I had looked. I could not write, I could not read. I could do nothing but wait. All functioning seemed suspended. I learned something of the marvelous personality of Time—how hindered, blocked, balked every way, even almost completely halted, it nevertheless persists in filtering quietly through man's obstructions, as if to say that nothing can be really effective against it. Slowly, of incalculable torpidity, it does still always and invariably though ever so imperceptibly, move. Fifteen minutes was my only friend —to get through fifteen minutes at a time, and then to get through another fifteen minutes and see by the clock that it too had gone by, was my only route to living again. Of course I too was ill, but that was unimportant. I would be well enough again when she came.

CHAPTER X   *To Bart*

AND then the paradise that followed that! Not at first—I was too numb to take her to me. I hardly knew that it had really happened, that she was there again in the chair by me. I was in a kind of mental paralysis. I could only dumbly look at her where she sat in agonized suspension waiting for my winter to dissolve. But soon, for a few immortal weeks, it was a miracle of joy that came home to me every evening.

We began now at last to live some of the life of our love. We felt our way, slowly, into the heart of its enchantment. Our love was an atmosphere in which we existed, in which all we did or said took place. It was a climate in which we could happily spread out, join our intellectual and aesthetic interests, and garner our mutual treasures for memory. How shall I say even a little of all we learned in our discoveries? We were two who had each an especial capacity for beauty-loving, each an almost painful sense for the poetry of life. For our time we had each lived much and fiercely and been through the deep waters of the soul. And we were desperately, magnificently, toweringly in love. The infinite potentialities of it staggered us; our incredible luck, the portentous unheard-of magnitude of what we had, terrified and overwhelmed us like some tidal wave. It consecrated us to great things. We felt it to be making us and we were passionately resolved it should make us aright.

That period also was when we first were able to gratify our longing to be outdoors together. Outdoors always quickened our perception of each other, wrought in us to create more kinds of joy for one another. I can feel her warm lips contrasted with her cold pungent cheek as she drove me up a long winding hilly road to where there was a great reach of view. Another day we let ourselves through bars from one upland sun-drenched field to another until habitations were left far behind and no human evidences were visible from the open hill-top where we picnicked and loved and lay. What happiness the human heart is capable of! We always longed to have the earth under us instead of a bed. Earth felt so good to us, so favorable, so part of us. We wanted to be absorbed by outdoors, to be one with weathers and animals and all vegetation. Once in the rain, under a big umbrella, we stood in a tangled soaking garden path and watched a dark, wet, delicious, earthy hollow under a low tree, hidden all with creepers dripping, and were devoured with our longing to be naked there. We had ties, and we risked no pneumonia, but we both loved rain. One rainy Sunday we went to a beautiful deserted plantation, and that day did achieve a part of our ambition for freedom. We became as nearly wild as two responsible things in civilization can. We played with tree-trunks and rain and wet grassy slopes, and leaped and climbed and lay. We had dressed warmly enough to be able to forget ourselves. We ran, we chased, we drank the delicious contrast of warm lips and cold rain, of earth-wetted, chilled face and warmed bosom.

As for talk, there was a never-ending flow between us. Some chatter no doubt, but also thought, such as we had, such as we minted under pressure of great experience. It was our whole inner selves

made articulate. Whether well or ill we had to trans-
fer ourselves into the medium of exchange. As her
hand lay upon me in loving unity I would begin to
speak, making my response to it in sentences. While
I sought the mirror of feeling and hunted the perfect word-combination, we opened the gates to idea
and explored the byways of perception wherever
they might lead. All inquiry was our province, but
the aesthetic speculation that was opened to us
seemed the very attribute of our mutual life. Love
never created thought more spontaneously.

Ah, those were weeks of wonder. They became at
length and by slow degrees a full-blooming of fulfillment. In our unvisited comfortless retreat, after the
parenthesis of Elaine's daily correspondence had received Rachel's attention and been closed, the evenings opening into night were hours of enchantment. No purer or more beautiful initiation into
sense can ever have been lived. For myself I knew
without hesitation that this was the height of life for
me. Without the resources of the ordinarily married
our transports were of a more exalted nature. To
man and woman come their climaxes that subside
again. The urgency to union follows a preordained

road and fulfillment has finality in it. Woman and woman, if they feel suction toward each other, must unite in the realm of the wish and the spirit, with in consequence a vastly greater stretch of the capacities. The search for ways of sealing marriage of heart and soul became for us an imaginative play of a very special order. Pressure of need to identify oneself in the other obliges new channels, new means, to be created. The imagination and the mind's ambition are what are continuously fed, instead of the womb whose claim dies whenever it is met. A passion in solution, never precipitated, must be its own genius. The unforeseen inspirations of ours were what came to be the bible of my retrospect.

Such a passion is pure, in the specialized sense of that word. How many times have I wished it had a fleshly end! "If I may only some way pay," I moaned, "give in return somehow my share of the world's suffering in exchange for this heavenly blessing that is mine, these holy unspeakable joys!" A wife, in the exaltation of true mating, may welcome the travail-pangs in such a mood. We knew we should have to pay in sacrifice probably, and did we not!—but we longed for a more creative fruition, and envied those that have the appointed ordinance of making a child out of their love. In defáult of that we dedicated ourselves to other ambitions, and lived in a rarefied atmosphere of high purpose. I suppose we were never so creditable in all our ways, as during those years when we had each other to live up to.

It was in that time of delight after frustration that I was released enough to send the message I spoke of to my beloved friend Sarah, she whose sense for life and drama had matched mine since my early youth. Hitherto our adventures had been hand in hand, all our reactions open to each other. "What I think of you most often for just now," I wrote Sarah, "is in my desire that you should share with me and appreciate this treasure that I have at present appropriated —treasure of poetic understanding, of delicate honor, of thirst after life and capacity for it. I have been meeting with the greatest experience of my life so far, in the shape,—strangely, oh, believe me strangely enough,—of another woman. I am safe though, in asking your trust? When two women become as ardent about each other as Rachel and I, the usual inference, I know, is that there is something ignoble about it. But your confidence in me, your trust, is imperative to me. One thing you will be glad of, with me: Knowing the apotheosis of interfeminine love has removed entirely for me the thrust of the man-question, without in the smallest degree affecting the purely feminine nature of the love. I regard the possible experience of marriage now quite differently and much more sensibly. Indeed at the moment I see all life with more equanimity, as from the top of the hill when you have climbed there you can get proportions and perspective as you can't when still struggling up. I have seen interfeminine love when I despised it. But we two are beset with the belief that no two have ever loved as we—certainly no two women. I at least have attained a warmth of personal joy and content I didn't dream possible for me. I can believe again in my own potentialities, can look now to turn the creative force that is in any great love into some channel of worthwhile activity."

But this structure of happiness out of which I wrote so confidently to Sarah lasted a month only and then crashed again. The struggle was now just beginning, the struggle for the right to our very intercourse as friends, that was waged, with repeated alternations of hope and its shattering, for the following many months. Elaine in the sanitarium was once more very ill. The doctor frankly summoned Rachel and she had to go. When Rachel answered such a summons it was something in the spirit in which man goes forth to war. She could soothe the patient. She was needed, could be successful in an urgent cause; she had made trouble enough and here she could be justified by works. I would wait for her; she had me and could wear me in her heart, and meantime if she must go we would make our sacrifice in the name of service. And in fact this parting had not in it that terrible strain when youth is deprived of its goal, unfinished and unfulfilled, that had been in our separation during Elaine's presence under our roof, or that constituted my anguish after their departure for New York. We were in a less distracted frame of mind and could resume if we had to, in some confidence and still greater abandonment, the diet of the mail.

It became evident after a time that no return to our refuge was to be thought of for Rachel if Elaine was to be got back to normal, so I too bade good-bye to the colonial brick porch ("brick brought from

England" as the poor old man who owned it told us so many times), to the oil-lamp and the high ceiling under which love and agony had taken turns. I went back to Rachel's home county where she must come sooner or later, and took quarters not near but near enough so that we could have the immediate advantage of opportunity if any offered. And there I lived out the waiting months of Elaine's slow convalescence while Rachel was back in Washington.

But when finally Elaine, much improved, was happily brought down to stay with the family for the summer, I might have been a thousand miles away for all the use it was to us. The mere sight of a letter arriving in my handwriting was enough to set the old vicious wheel revolving. To plan a meeting was to cause a crisis at once, all the benefit of the sanitarium months undone. Elaine was waging war in earnest now, a performance compared to which her previous efforts had been only desultory. As long as Rachel held out for her right to love where she pleased, Elaine could not stem the onsets of despair that would lead up to the nervous crises. Nowadays it would be dealt with as a psychosis and other people perhaps saved from sacrifice to it. But the doctor had long since made it clear to Rachel that her cousin's sanity and probably her life were dependent on her.

And Rachel would surrender everything but her right. While it was evidently necessary she would refrain from seeing me, but she would hope it would not always be necessary, and meantime she would certainly not deprive herself or me of letters.

CHAPTER XI *To Bart*

MUCH time passed like this, time of grief on every side. I needn't dwell on the developments, always in a circle, during that summer. Elaine's condition was agitating all their group, and there we all were at a deadlock, and time not only doing no good, but making her condition slowly worse. The continued separation that was costing the two of us so much was not accomplishing anything for anyone, and for us it was only aggravated by the rare moment of re-union which suffered amputation again as soon as the blood began to flow through it. Worn down at last, we came to perceive that there was probably nothing else to do but surrender. If a life or sanity were likely to be forfeited by our persisting in hoping for each other, even though we stayed many miles apart, if actually that absurdity were true, there was no escape from the logic of the case. One other alternative there indeed was. But I could not exactly remain a few miles away, waiting for the pathological body to cease to function, though that course was the one urged upon me by no less a person than my own doctor. No, if Elaine were likely to die, or go over the mental borderline, I had to be clear in my own mind as to my possible responsibility. We had better admit that we could not go on with the risk. Not agreeing not to love—that was an impossibility—we finally agreed that we would do for Elaine the most that we were able, that is, that we would separate completely. We would neither write nor hear, nor hope to meet. We would in short renounce. For Elaine we would give each other up.

I marvel now that we should have come to it. But I could never give you an understandable account of the wearing-down process for both Rachel and me that there was in the morbid Elaine's tenacious insistence. It was so cruel as it was that there could hardly be any more cruelty in sacrificing everything. The decision painfully reached, with full sense of what it meant for us, all manner of final arrangements were begun, final information exchanged, books returned, a multitude of small affairs wound up in one way or another. Half measures would have been impossible to maintain, and half measures would have been no better than none for the Elaine whose peace required the severing of all relations. We had the poor comfort of knowing that ours was the better part. The ridiculous and cruel business was to be consummated in all good faith, the date set when all lines would be considered cut. The day came, the last choked word was finally exchanged, and the descent to Avernus begun. Such futilities are in order when so sick a person rules.

Of course nothing came of the renunciation, causing so much anguish and executed in such sincerity. A telegram came within a few days saying that the last state was worse than the first, that the invalid could not endure what she had done. Well, there were but the two alternatives: either she must benefit by the divorcement she had brought about, or she must suffer the attachment and consent to bear the consequences. It goes without saying that no serious consequences came. At last accounts Elaine was still living and well. She had entirely recovered from the long mental trouble of her earlier life. But that did not occur until I, for a far other reason, had dropped finally out of her Rachel's existence.

Meantime, since there seemed to be no rational course for us, either in heaven or hell, and nothing could be gained by awaiting the issue in limitless frustration, I set about removing from the vicinity the scourge that I had apparently become. I made my arrangements to put the ocean between us. Facing therefore a separation without term and without hope, we gave ourselves some last painful opportunities for comfort. Once, being hard driven with her troubles, my Rachel broke away from them in desperation, rode the intervening miles to me and sat between my knees, putting her head back between my breasts. We could scarcely speak, and we parted again without relief. Again, an accident achieved a night for us together. When we were awakened in the morning, we had just dropped off to sleep. As was usually the case after the long starvations, we had not thought of sleep all night. We spent the last two days and nights, in torment and bliss, together.

My long journey further and further away from the beloved was enveloped by her. I was dedicated.

Either is Love

I was a nun. I was no one's, least of all my own. I was hers indefeasibly, the property of her unlocking hands, which had sealed up my passional life. For a time I had my little lip-bruises, a tiny dark spot or two that were her last signature upon me. Not for long however,—even that trace vanished. And I had her pictures. I cannot allege the usual lover's plaint that pictures do not do justice to the loved one. To me those pictures among them perfectly represented her. I could not have them much about—I was made weak if I looked at them too long. They were kept out of sight, one for one need, one for another.

Forbidden any connection but the one by mail, we expanded that one with all the thwarted ardor of our souls. We made of written correspondence a phenomenon comparable in intensity of the imagination to the physical one we had laid down. I cannot deny that our record, if alive today, or fifty years from today, would be something of moment. The written association between two active-minded and trusting people in love is more than a mere series of answered letters. It is a different intercourse from the oral one; it has different virtues. A self-winding mechanism, once set in motion, it cannot be ar-

rested without violence. So many things combine in
it—the narrative of events and the response on all of
that; the unburdening of the consciousness in solil-
oquy; conversation, with the handicap of the long
waits between question and answer, or between comment and comment; and of course lovemaking
which is of such an insidious kind in letters. The
necessary technique of such correspondence educates
the imagination and disciplines the quality of tolerance. Keeping clear of the inevitable annoyances in
a complicated chain of communication is something
of an undertaking where only two or three days
elapse between a letter and the answer it provokes.
But where two weeks intervene, the strain is so great
that most letter-writing is seriously lamed by it. Its
removal from immediacy taxes faith and memory
too much. Ah, I know a great deal about it. For we
learned how to survive all that; our connection never
languished. Though in the constant series we sent
across the water,—each of us a thick envelope-full
nearly every day,—every letter crossed several others
coming, so that sequence of discussion was annihi-
lated and some important matter was always at cross-
purposes between us, still the passion-channel always

was open, and that we competed joyously to keep so. The transatlantic mailbag can never have contained more incendiary matter than we put into it with all the suggestion that we could kindle at the pencil-point. Some of that lovemaking in the packages of letters that accumulated so fast in my trunk was remarkable. And its humor never failed. Rachel was entertainment always—no matter when or where.

My departure was the signal of course for Elaine to improve in health, Elaine who was so sure there was no jealousy in her, who had clung to that asseveration through thick and thin, though all else should be lost. Oh, yes, she improved in health. And after that long winter of my secluded life in Vienna—outer mind filled with the effort of sustained writing, and inner one with the thirst for which the only alleviation was the American mail —what do you suppose happened? Fate took a hand.

One day in spring, as I was ascending my staircase, a telegram was passed to me. I had the sudden exalted sense that it contained momentous news that was good, but I reached the top of the third flight and put some coal in my stove before I put that pre-

vision to the test. And then I read. And there stood
the heavenly visitant. Imbedded in the few crisp
words of the cable lay the facts I easily caught because I knew the circumstances, that Rachel's depart-
ment was sending her to England, had appointed
her to a short mission in London. And that she had
secured a leave of absence in addition which would
give her some months on the continent for an investigation that had been an ambition of hers. There
it was. Our franchise. For me the world changed
from then on.

You say you know how to wait. I know something about waiting myself. If one is well, one can
throw one's thoughts away from it, but underneath
is the expectancy going on; at best it is likely to be
a feat of endurance, even with the prospect of re-
ward. There were still some weeks to be got through
before she would arrive in Southampton, and I felt
bound to carry out a promise I had made to take an
older relative just at that time for a little trip in
Switzerland. And that I did, without too bad grace
I hope, in my secret happiness of anticipation. So
that after all I was not on the dock to take her to
me, and our transports were not mixed with the

work to be accomplished in London. It was fully three weeks afterward that we finally made our conjunction, which was prosaically effected at a railroad station in Paris.

CHAPTER XII *To Bart*

IT was a painful ecstasy. For some two or three nights, neither of us could sleep. Only to be in one another's presence was violent excitement. But that furious tension gradually relaxed of course in the amazing consciousness that at last we were companions, without pressure from any direction. Isolation from all claims was so unheard of for us that it was like moving in a foreign element, not yet quite to be really counted on. To spend all day together and then all night and all next day again with no limit threatening us, created a calm to float in that we had never known. We had not only time for ourselves alone, but we began to have time to sightsee and better yet to read about what we were seeing. We had, as weeks together moved into months, time to seek out and be with the people we liked, and miracle of miracles, we had time to waste in the rest we so much needed. As to what we wanted to do together, the possibilities were dizzying. We projected various achievements. We had only to be permitted to come together naturally, when our energy turned at once into objective channels.

I had the satisfaction of seeing Rachel received by all my friends with appreciative delight. The pleasant experiences and amusing adventures and contacts we piled up, the unmitigated joy we took in everyone and everything we saw and whatever we did,—if I should begin to recite any of it I should never finish the story. What we saw was after all very little of "abroad" as such; it was our acquaintances and the European setting reflected through each other's eyes. Being in love is mostly a way of looking at the world. We were consumingly content. Everything was understood between us. Our needs were filled. It was thorough, irremediable, all-embracing. We were one, without ever becoming so; we were just born that way.

So I pass over all the enchantment of that perfect time. It fled in a riot of happiness. At last we had everything. We showed ourselves what we could do with it when we had it. I remember how we used to uncoil and fling apart in our big old-fashioned bed when we heard the femme de ménage coming to make up our fire, and spend the half-hour while the room was warming up in a contemplation of all the felicities from which we could choose, like epicures, for the day. Once we had the fun of bathing in a huge tub together—we were so pleased over the opportunity and so worshipful with it. She had gained a little in weight when she came to me, to my surprise and slight shock, for it did affect that curving line of perfect profile that I found so devastating. On the other hand it had given the boyish chest a new rounding that went utterly to my head, as I could almost believe it was my coaxing of the feminine in her that was responsible for it. How could there have been any pseudo-masculine there, when I wanted her as feminine as possible? I wanted to teach her and clothe her and sophisticate her powers. Me she had completely captivated; what could she not do, I thought, with a few men about, and a growing interest in the matter. We were too much absorbed to look for other excitement. But had she not been preoccupied, wakened as she was, I believe no man could have looked into those laughter-shot sea-blue eyes unstirred. I still fail to understand why no man has ever succumbed to that intense charm, if none has. The men we met always liked her.

It is a marvel to me now that we could work at anything else when so much of our attention was invested in each other. But she did do a very interesting piece of investigation—rather an achievement —during that time. The work of a bureau has since been built on that beginning. And in my own very different realm she helped me with my problems to such a degree that my understanding of what I was doing grew as by magic. We helped to build one another. We mutually admired and believed in and encouraged the best in our differing talents. Each considered the other little short of a genius. Even for those who are a good deal distracted by passion, it is a favorable atmosphere for accomplishment.

I had no idea when I was called down to Cannes by my brother Roger's illness that it would be so long before I should get back to her, and that by then our time together should have had its death-blow, again through the agency of the old antagonist. During our period of freedom and light, Elaine at home had suddenly expanded resources. She had been the happy beneficiary of a legacy. When this news became known, her doctor, who it seemed to me was always too ready to pass his responsibility on to Rachel, at once urged upon her cousin the project of a vacation abroad. What more convenient, since Rachel was already there? The project required an extension of Rachel's leave of course, and Rachel did some adventurous cabling and secured it. I was in Cannes while the matter was being decided. I could not leave Roger to pneumonia or even to convalescence alone, and week followed week toward the date of Elaine's arrival while I simmered helplessly over Roger's trays and Rachel worked frantically to finish the Paris inquiry and get to me if I could not get to her. My nights were distraught, my days spent straining after signs of my patient's improvement. I have often wondered how Roger interpreted the acuteness of my concern for him. He never showed any astonishment.

Of course we had enjoyed a long term of privilege and should be ready with decent grace to submit to Elaine's turn in the sun. I did not begrudge her the prospect, but to lose the final weeks that we were entitled to, with the old familiar specter of permanent parting once more menacing us, was almost not to be borne. When at length I was able to see my patient into good hands and fly to rejoin my lover, Elaine had already landed and was in London. Rachel had thought a week's delay in reaching her would not be serious, and telegrams were coming and going. Elaine was gracious, but she was there waiting, and a message shortly came reporting fresh illness weathered alone in the London hotel. The old weary problem and risk. Even though the risk were imaginary or superinduced or neurotic or what you will, there it was, and we could not take an hour's ease. Another telegram implored Rachel to come at once, and shortened our last reunion to three days only.

They were days of happiness shot through with pain, I might say of pain in which there was yet some happiness. And in that passionate reunion after hunger, in our desperate snatching at whatever we could get before the separation that seemed to have finality in it, I became somehow dimly aware that also between ourselves, fundamentally, all was not right.

How to describe it? You know how in speaking or in writing, some good phrase, we'll say, spurts up out of your welling need. It is a good phrase, helpful for your purpose, and remains there in your brain. Next time you speak of the same thing you repeat the same phrase, because it saves effort, and because it is expressive. And then the next time, to someone else, you say the same words to cover the same idea. And each time you use that phrase it is a little falser, because emotion has not produced it, only memory. When you first said it, it was sincerity itself. But to keep on using it makes it as insincere as guile.

So in love. The act that meets the emotional need of the moment belongs to that moment only of all time. If repeated for its own sake out of memory, it is falsified. Yet once the brain-registrations have been made, the nerve-centers will definitely ask for repetition of their sensations. To be a great lover is to respond freshly moment by moment to the infinite shadings and temperatures at the heart of love, something no worried person can do well, nor yet a satiated person. Straining to hoard all we could against a hungry future we were using touch-coinage that was not newly minted. I was giving and taking, not what I had inevitably to give and take, but what

Either is Love

I was in the habit of giving and taking. It was the best I could do under the circumstances, but the circumstances were our enemy. If there is not time to wait for fresh germination and some little act has once been the sum of life's rapture, will that little act itself not supply the rapture again? We had to seize while we might all that we had ever seized, whether or not desire was at the exact tension for it. In that I recognize now the seed of subsequent disaster. Once before when in despair at parting, I had been conscious of something not strictly ours combating the maintenance of truth in our most delicate relations. It was the first faintly floating straw in that wind that afterward blew out our flame. Constant companionship had rescued us during our long months of reunion. Our attention was filled with navigating the strong current of our joy. But with the starvation-element restored and crisis upon us, what we did, unknowing, was to injure the perfect fitting of expression to ardor, which had been the great achievement of our love. I have reason to think that her ardor during those last moments in Paris was as it had ever been, but that I was too weary, too disappointed, too bogged down in the perplexities, to be quite in unison with her. We separated unappeased, unhoping. That Rachel might join and take care of her cousin, as formerly, we tore ourselves apart.

The cousin had a holiday of much delight. She developed distinguished connections in England, who supplied for Rachel and herself some highly interesting experiences. I went back to Vienna. After a time Roger came and we took our little flat. I did most of my second book that winter and planned my third. When my contract came it tied me to Europe for some time. Since we might not marry and have done with any disputing of our claims, no future that would allow us a life together could be descried except by the dogged inner eye of hope.

CHAPTER XIII   *To Bart*

DO you believe with me in the indissolubility of Love and Grief? That there is an affinity that draws these two inexorably together, no matter how favorable are circumstances to keep them apart? Has love ever lived out its life without the other visitation? By its very presence Love lays the heart open to suffering, though it had never been vulnerable before. The proportions of joy and torment seem to be in delicate balance. Most fulfilled desire has had its probation of longing, of hope deferred, or of doubt. It is a distinguished passion that has never known loss of faith, loss of admiration, or loss of the loved one himself. Would Dante's devotion never have been clouded—I have often wondered—if an actual life with his beloved had been begun? You and I have the principle to test, if we end by joining our roads. Rachel knew. She had tried to tell me at the beginning, in her first halting letter with the beautiful handwriting, to beg me to be warned off, not to love her. She sat by her river and implored me to consider my risk before becoming involved with her. But even had I foreseen—love is of such value that one gladly embraces the risks. Even when grief has arrived, one would not erase the experience.

In the very week that had taken her away from me she had her first momentary defection. Not in fact a defection—she briefly looked another way. It amazed her beyond describing. She wrote about it at length—how she had been swept off her feet by the beauty and youth of a girl in the hotel, had been distinctly aware of temptation, inexplicable, to let the child's young bewildered desire increase, and had finally shaken her off some days later. I thought little of it; it touched me in no way.

Next, she wrote of having left a packet of my letters in a drawer and being unable to get them back. Also, nothing. But still my letters had been like her heart's blood, detaching herself from them impossible to conceive. I was as conscious of her letters in a room as I could be of a person. Mine had been like sentient life for her.

It was only after her journey home across the

water and we had re-established our line of communication, when she was now plunged in fresh
work so remote from me, that I began by degrees
to have any real uneasiness. Her new work was
executive in character; one Anna, a friend of long
standing, was her immediate assistant and companion that winter, and I came to sense omissions and
lapses in the accounts of their week-ends taken together. And then she confessed to me that Anna
had become in my absence a temptation to her, that
long kisses were not unknown to them, yet that
Anna's province was wholly different from mine
and in no way affected our complete union, etc.
After that, confessions about Anna were less full. I
kept my discomfort out of my letters. Our chain of
intercourse did not really suffer; at least the episode
of Anna did not perceptibly injure it. We were too
great a habit with each other. Her letters were always full of people. She had many enthusiasms.
New people were often an excitement to her—new
people were to me—and I could not be jealous of
them all.

Then ultimately, a long time later, Rachel was
put into a highly responsible and commanding posi-

tion. It was a rapid rise in a rapidly expanding field, and all Rachel's faculties were challenged by it. She had the ability for the work, the leadership involved, the organizing and selection of human material, as well as understanding and pleasure in the scientific nature of it. I could only hold my breath and rejoice, though I watched with some anxiety, from afar. She was still the fundamental fact in my life, and I in hers. But now I perceived that the Martha who was a new associate, had fallen a victim, and Rachel, it was apparent, was finding Martha extremely necessary to her in all she was doing. If Rachel had a professional trip to make, Martha must go with her. If Martha were ill, Rachel must stay with her, and so on. And so on. Still I was to be sure that no one encroached on the inner preserves where I remained supreme as always. These were people who needed her, she explained, who palliated her loneliness for me. But she was profoundly disturbed—she showed it—over her own capacity to receive new people into her love, love with more desire in it than either Martha or Anna had ever suspected was possible to them, but still to Rachel only an echo of what she carried in her bosom. I understand it. I even understood it then. It comes back to the question of expression. Having established certain habits in connection with affection, the habits automatically assert themselves whenever affection arises. Yet in my case that logic had not operated; no one else has ever approached the territory that Rachel pre-empted in me, and I believe my friendships with women have been remarkably rich and permanent.

Rachel did not know what to think of this willingness of hers to touch these others in desire, and in the end she came to revile herself for it. She underwent disillusion and loss of faith in herself over it, and broke the hearts, incidentally, of both Martha and Anna. The Rachels of the world are the sufferers—those people to whom passionate love is necessary and who are also sensitized to honor. Rachel's sanity was saved by her resiliency. But she couldn't forgive herself for the pain she had dealt out to both those people, and when Ruth appeared, Ruth the new friend who set her face sternly against all physical manifestations whatsoever as between women, and was able to maintain that standard regardless of the powerful pull that she herself felt toward Rachel, Rachel went over to her way of thinking in a kind of passion of relief and expiation. In taking the communion in a church whither Ruth, gayish sort of bird though she was, had led her, she put away in one act of renunciation all dealings with women's love forevermore. I didn't quite know that—she didn't break it to me in so many words. What happened was that, torn between her emotions and her misgivings, she began to fail to write me at all.

Friendship is seldom saved out of the wreck of a love-affair. But in our case as a pair of reasoning women, why could we not have preserved our friendship?

Always during separation our most imperative need was the outlet by letter. No matter how crowded were Rachel's days, the instant of her relaxation was my instant and she flew to me in it, either by penciled scratchings on whatever was handy or by prolonged outpourings in form. She could hardly wait for her opportunity. But after the European interlude the chain became less reliable. She was busy, outrageously busy, too busy to "accomplish any letters." Explaining at length the reasons which prevented her from securing time to write left relatively little of it for writing itself. So that my knowledge of her became much less full. And then much less full. I easily guessed that her need of love and understanding was being a good deal supplied at close hand, and after the advent of Ruth, very well supplied indeed. I did not interpret Ruth as in any sense a destroyer. If Rachel had acquired wisdom through her, I wanted access to that wisdom too. Ruth was a person who carried gallantly some heavy responsibilities, I understood, and she must have had much character. Her hold upon Rachel, I firmly believe, was in the fact that she refused Rachel's demonstrative advances. If some such refusal were the next step for us, I was ready to be shown too. We had our store of memories which nothing could tarnish. Ruth knew God well and had introduced Rachel to him, a powerful contact of course and one that I would gladly have aspired to for myself. And what between the absorption in God and the absorption in Ruth to take what time was left from work, I got a good deal neglected.

You have spoken of being somewhat strung up when four days have passed without a letter from me. In three months, the autumn after my own return to America, I had a total of four letters from Rachel. Mere obligation never spelt letter-writing to her. She would have felt a greater humiliation, quite rightly, in writing me out of duty than in not writing me at all. I refrained, by applying all the self-restraint I had, from sending her many more letters than I received. And when I did write, I could not be honest, and it was an anguish of make-believe cheer that nearly wiped me out each time. To this day I am glad to remember that I never wrote to her—never—a word of reproach nor a syllable of claim. I had Elaine's contrary policy seared into my recollection. If she went from me I made not the slightest struggle to keep her. But strung-up is inadequate; I was thoroughly wrung that winter. It was slow torture to hope and watch the mails, day after day, in vain. There was not only the suffering for what I was myself losing, but I felt acutely the unnecessary loss to her. She valued her connection with me and what it had brought her, valued it enormously, but it was very like her not to let that motive or any other take the place of the pure and personal passion there had been. For some years I had been used to turning in her direction with a sunflowery fixity, and as month followed month of darkness I was so reduced that I should have been willing to accept any motive whatever, even that of her obligation to me, or her pity, for the sake of news of her. I remember sending her an expensive present at Christmas, something I knew she would like but really beyond my means, solely to buy from her some note of acknowledgment. Could there have been a steeper descent? I only did that once. The act had no genuineness in it but that of last resort. Whereas her going from me was as undiluted in its integrity and as genuine as her coming to me had been.

CHAPTER XIV

ONLY, if she went, she went. Love requires nourishment like any other living thing. Conversely, if given poison, it must suffer in its health. Enough poisonous food, enough perfidy or bad behavior, will kill it. Or enough starvation. To admire is at the root of all loving. The lover *must* admire. I was obliged to see that what she was doing was not admirable—slowly killing the heart of me whom she had regarded as part of herself; it shocked me. I would not ask for that food that was formerly so abounding. In fact it was not there for me any longer. But the pain, due to famishment, that overtook me every night and a dozen times during the day, inevitably affected my regard for her. In that year of neglect she lost me. She simply would not find me there again; I would have changed. My only course was to change. I did change. I did violence to my love of her. Rather than let my living

138

passion die of gradual starvation, I deliberately put out its life. I choked the thought of her. I throttled my inclination toward her. I closed my inner door and left her on the outside. I threw her again and again from my threshold until my mental habits could do without her. But not without paroxysms of grief with every renewed effort.

Gradually that winter I made a separation of her into two. It was a device that worked itself out in me for a kind of automatic protection. One of the two was that attractive young woman the outer Rachel, known to my friends, she of the yellow hair, the compelling personality and the place in the world, the talking, moving, working, potent creature who had so many good stories and such a contagious laugh, the one who had been abroad with me and now had the notable position in Washington, and from whom, I could say quite casually if asked, that I was hearing very rarely now because she was so busy. For her I was engaged in strangling my love, over and over, as often as I caught it living. The other was a very different being, the image that dwelt within my most sacred treasure-house of recollection, of which none could deprive me and on

which even in crucifixion I could feed day and night.
I did feed on it—it sustained me still as it had done
for years. I could even sleep in it—by invoking the
spirit of it to surround me, I could sink into the
feeling of her and sleep. In ineffable moments I had
cried out, "All the suffering I can ever have could
not balance this paradise of now," and those moments were mine yet, they were no one else's. I had
lived them; they were wrought into me. I was rich
of them forever. Alone, I could withdraw into the
province where she—it—was, and distill afresh the
essence, relive the happiness, and return to my outer
life refreshed and at peace. But the living young
woman my late companion was not a part of that in-
ward provision—she had flown from it. To her I was
never fully wedded after we separated in the south
of France.

It was during that winter that I extracted from
her the destruction of the written record. Lovers who
have had continuous access to each other during
their courtship period do not have such records. But
lovers who have to love by letter have a body of testi-
mony, if they will, till the end of their days. Since
the pain lay over ours, my trunkful was like the

murdered corpse—I could not look at it, and I could not let it alone. I saw that the record had to go, else peace could never be again. I knew the worth of that correspondence if only as literature, and it was also material of value to human science, if ever in the course of time such an alliance as ours should come to be analyzed and understood. As that time had not come yet, the record was too subject to mischance, and it had to be extinguished. She was not as sure as I of the necessity, but she conceded my right to the request, and the whole mass, as it existed in two places, was destroyed.

Before the dividing process I have mentioned was altogether complete, and seven years after that spring when we had first drunk of the elixir, there came an opportune time for me to put the whole painful uncertainty to a final test. It seemed as if a little plain understanding might help the liquidation for us both, even though the liquidation itself was inevitable. What I did was to write her inviting her to travel with me once more for a short vacation. I suggested to her several interesting possibilities which had at one time or another been joint dreams of ours. Save for my overpowering distress it should have been a happy program. It brought her. She got herself free, and she came.

I believe the woman was actually surprised at the state of pain she found me in. What had happened —it was plain—was that she had been too absorbed in her own rapid developments to think very far into my probable condition. I had managed not to betray much of it at long distance. One cause of her failing me, moreover, was the very sense of doing so which paralyzed her. I had not realized in the scanty accounts I had had of her mental movements that her religious awakening was related to her letting me go. She had hardly formulated even to herself what that awakening was to do in any connection. But when we had talked a little, I learned in devastating horror, what had not hitherto once entered my head, that she had been including in her rejections the nature of our mutual love! That to me most sacred, life-giving, overwhelmingly beautiful and spiritual expression of living poetry, our mutual love—she had been questioning its nature. Questioning it! The outrage which that brought to the tenderest center of my being, when I heard it and took it in, sundered us instantly and forever. It made the de-

cree absolute. Myself, my inner precinct, was henceforth mine alone. Our mutual memories were no
longer hers—they were only mine, to live with and
protect as I saw fit; she, least of all she, might not
approach anywhere near them. I should be happy to
retain the interesting Rachel as companion and
friend, but that person bore no degree of relation
whatever to the lover who still occupied my heart,
though dead.

Long afterwards in some isolated letter she
humbly repented that ill-omened premature judging
of hers of our great mutual passion. She could not
comprehend her confusion about it; it was so plainly
by then the best gift God had ever made her, and
known to her for that. Too late. The best I could do
for that belated retraction was silence. The damage
was long since done; it could not be undone. There
is no going back.

Out of our trip that spring she did manage to
wrest, characteristically, plenty of interest and adventure in spite of the constant flowing accompani-
ment of my tears, which rained whenever our
trouble was under consideration and almost whenever it wasn't. For one thing we were no longer

united as lovers; we had separate rooms. This alone was grief—grief for lost beauty, and grief for what must yet be gone through before years could cure me of longing. For another, whenever we were able to take to our familiar loved outdoors, I inevitably spoiled the face of nature by weeping upon it. I couldn't control my tears—my grief would have me by the throat whenever I looked at her, whether outdoors or in. She was a live reminder of happiness now lost, and the sight of it would finish me afresh. She would glance up from some jovial narrative while packing, or while lunching, or while waiting for a train, to find me dissolved again. I was anything but a cheerful companion, and it exasperated me that I should invite a guest and then persistently destroy her pleasure. She bore it very well of course. She always had philosophy. She felt very sorry about it all and somehow guilty, and was very kind and protecting, and she very tactfully enjoyed everything as thoroughly as she could in order to help me out.

When it was all over and a last gallant gesture of the hand came back to me on the station platform, I passed that summer in a state of exhaustion. I remember how I used to sit speechless with my head back, eyes shut but filtering tears as usual, trying to gather strength enough to get upstairs to my room. I wonder my relatives endured me. They laid my discouragement to my health, which was in fact bad enough to take all the blame. That I was merely broken-hearted was something that never crossed their minds.

When I had an operation that fall I recall the acute irony that there was for me in all the overflowing sympathy over it—such a nothing as it was. The flowers flooding my hospital room, the kindly notes and good wishes, the duty my friends made of coming in to see me. I could more easily have undergone five such operations than the amputation that was going on in my soul. But sympathy was an anesthetic that that other surgical interference never had.

Very slowly, very, very gradually, time began by degrees and surreptitiously to make things a little less bad for me, as time is bound to do. The sting would be less constant, and after a long while my heartache would consent to stay below the surface for considerable periods, when I could work again.

Either is Love

Then it would rise to the rim of my self-containment once more and I would have to vanish out of my world for a time until the violence of the storm had again washed down the accumulations of grief. With the best of intentions the creature would swell my anguish by little presents which would come in the mail from time to time. In the prime of our fervor we had never exchanged gifts, probably because it was Elaine's custom to rain presents on her Rachel, and I had seen what a nuisance and embarrassment they could be. Rachel hated the habit, and it was a special understanding between us that we did not need tokens when we had the whole of each other. We had liked our capacity to abstain from giving things, who gave life instead. Presents now only underscored our abdication of Olympus. I could not endure them and could not stop her from this substitute for a letter that she would occasionally think of. I gave them away as fast as they came— got them out of sight without delay. A postcard would have been better than a dozen purchases. But no postcards ever came. And then even her annual letter ceased.

I do not even now understand the expression 'sinful' as I hear it in connection with love between women. I should not be likely to use the term in any case, because it is a churchly term, and I was not educated in a churchly environment and do not think of actions as sinful or not sinful. I should think sin was something that did harm in some form, to other people or of course to oneself. The excessive drinker does harm to his world as well as to himself. Lust demoralizes both participants, as well as injuring the possible unborn. Almost all the so-called sins can be interpreted in similar terms. But if women's love does not create tragedy for others, wherein does it harm? No child can be born. No bad habits can be bred. Ah, yes, if ecstasy is illegitimately induced; but that is lust. Lust can occur in any relation of life, lust for money, lust for power, as well as animal lust. Married life does not preclude it, God knows, and there are great numbers of extramarital forms. I can understand how lust might develop between women, and if that exists it is deplorable enough. But because incest occurs, is all family life vicious? Because there are brothels, is all sexual life unclean? A so-called Lesbian alliance can be of the most rarefied purity, and those who do not believe it are merely judging in ignorance of the facts.

What the whole issue came to in our case was the matter of satiety. Rachel has failed, one way or another, all the women for whom she has had impassioned love. This knowledge has been dreadful to her and in putting away passion, if that is what she did, she probably did the best and bravest thing. But I believe the beautiful and mysterious realm of touch need not be avoided when touch functions transcendently to make creative experience, and that if we could have left it at that we might have retained the high place of our love in our lives to this day. We had been united in the intention to keep alert to the direction of our sense-life, but constant harrying had numbed our critical capacity. Drought is never repaired by over-heavy rains; the famine victim cannot right his state by gluttony. Being defrauded, we grasped at last too voraciously, and so we forfeited the best thing that living had ever brought to either of us.

CHAPTER XV

THAT was the statement that I made for my husband before we came together. I had said at the beginning of my connection with Rachel that it would take me ten years to get over it. I was exactly prophetic, as it turned out. All the history of that early love, its groping uncharted growth, its unearthly beauty, its moral life and its equally moral suicide, had taken place in the span of ten years. Grief over it was all that was left me, and grief had long been the only guest with whom I shared my spiritual tenement. It was the night following a motor accident that the last and the most violent convulsion of that anguish occurred; and it was the motor accident that begot my friendship with the lonely man I afterwards married.

His wife and I had been taking a trip together out of convenience, hardly more at the outset than acquaintances. The shock of the disaster—I by some miracle unhurt, the companion of my trip in ghastly death beside me on the seat—all the horrors of that day and night until I could find the husband by telegraph and he could get to the poor little western town where it happened, and after that the spectacle of his pitiful high courage which I had not looked for, shook me to my foundations. But even all that, all the nightmare I had been through since our car left the highway, was not the real cause of the emotional flooding of that never-to-be-forgotten night. Like some hurricane that loosens old landmarks, the powerful terrors loosed in me by the tragedy were altogether those of my own ancient private grief. The paroxysms I underwent on my side of the partition in that small inconsequent hotel were all agonies of defeated love, the supreme violence of longing for my lost beautiful glory, the living food for my heart of which I was now starved. They were no kin of that other unimaginable despair in ignorance of mine; that he, the bereaved stranger enduring his own refinements of torture in the next cell, would some day assuage my despair and I his, was one of those strange chances of destiny that do not make sense. But it so proved. We were to end by re-creating the world for each other.

The me she had could not go to anyone else. As I told my husband long afterward, when he had a me it would be a different one, though her insignia would be upon it. Part of one goes; the lover who follows has to take what is left. My affectional nature was so spent, so impoverished, I was so dead to the appeal of love after that was over that I was doubtful if it could ever revive in me. But time is capable of making sensational changes. Perhaps grief calls to grief. At any rate mine began slowly to be discharged through the medium first of that new fellowship, and then in the absorbing life of the friendship and its vacillating progress in the course of time into something that had to be recognized as love. When the time came that I undertook to write for him the narrative of the rise and fall of my first love, ten years had been and gone since the blue-eyed young woman at the party had swallowed the strawberry out of the punch-glass.

And now again I am despoiled. But this confiscation of my happiness is in a different range of experience from that one. I am divested of something, but still there is a substance of some kind that can be grasped and held. The texture of that substance is real and it is not hurtful. It folds me about almost like an embrace, importunate and wistful, not abrasive, not stinging.

Quite recently I was taking a midnight train somewhere. I was hastening after my luggage along the platform when a sudden fresh sense of loss swept over me of almost fainting intensity for the moment. The hour, the rank coal-gas smell, the endless, stretching, looming Pullmans, all the dim, smoky, resounding night of the vast vaultless station came at me calling what my husband meant to me, my last lost advocate and friend. He was so large a factor in any going away, whether or not he went with me, his figure in its shell of heavy coat topped with a concealing hat carrying things for me through the din, as I ran along beside him, dodging trucks in the murk, keeping up with him, leaving everything to him. Unable to talk, hurrying only to locate the number of our car, how infinitely near, how dependent, how bound I was, how the turmoil enclosed us two in secret concert

152

extracting our purposes, our far goal of travel, out of present confusion and dark. I could suddenly smell and feel that large concealing coat of his passionately. There was something terribly moving in its rigidity of texture, its secretive impersonality, as if it were the very expression of his withdrawn self. But once within the warm stillness of the compartment with the porter's rustling gone, I would have unlocked its big buttons and blotted myself against the glasses case and so been held a few moments against all outside. Alone together—what a word-combination that is! Not an inch left between us.

Now under identical conditions he was strangely not there, not anywhere in the station. Though borne so vividly to me in the noise, the smell, the cold air and the concern to reach my distant goal of the Pullman, no one was there with my interests in his mind or knowing what they were, save a burdened little black figure in a red cap. Oh, where have you gone? I cried. Why did we have to part? We liked it so well to be together in what we did, to take trains together, to inhabit a house together, to eat dinners and study maps and plant bulbs together. I am still here doing those things. I need you, I look for you, I call.

I call, yes. I called there on the station platform in my heart. But at the same time I knew that the pain in that call is mitigated pain, is sweetened pain, growth pain perhaps. There is no wrong in it. Spear and vinegar have not entered it. Love is alive within it, not murdered, strangled, done to death. No trust has been violated, no tenderness outraged. My pain is part of a complex chemistry resolving, and what it will become lies in a not unfriendly future. I had had an intimation of that future, and I thought back to it and wrapped the cloak of it around me in my Pullman berth. It was like this:

A few days after my husband's sudden death I had had occasion to go up the village street at dusk to the house of an older man who lived alone. He had had a good wife and she was gone. Passing through his gate I thought he must be away as there was no light in the house. But as I set foot on the porch a window-glimmer shot me a silhouette across his firelight. It flashed for me the far distance ahead on the road of singleness I had just begun to travel. My neighbor was there. He was sitting by his hearth in a deep chair alone, his pipe the only sign of life. Here in the dusk he was waiting, probably quite unsentimentally in his familiar solitude, not in anguish, not in rebellion, but in appeasement and passivity. He rose to my knock without a touch of resentment at being interrupted in his loneliness. Peace like that was on the way to me too, I knew instantaneously as I stepped inside, though far off, infinitely far it seemed to me then, beclouded with my misery as I was. Love lived on like that in people with satisfying memories and continuing purposes. If there were dying in it, its dying was a metamorphosis gradual and merciful, the dignified dying that time itself contributes, as the dying of the foliage and the year. The accent shifts, only. Birth is implicit in the change, repudiation nowhere in the cycle. Love has been and was determining. It was full, it was long, it was contenting. It is not dead through death, but glows still as I saw it there in that friend's house, from a deep chair with a pipe, in favoring dusk beside a little fire licking itself up on burnished andirons.

HOMOSEXUALITY

Lesbians and Gay Men
in Society, History and Literature

Acosta, Mercedes de. **Here Lies The Heart.** 1960

Bannon, Ann. **I Am a Woman.** 1959

Bannon, Ann. **Journey To a Woman.** 1960

Bannon, Ann. **Odd Girl Out.** 1957

Bannon, Ann. **Women in The Shadows.** 1959

Barney, Natalie Clifford. **Aventures de L'Esprit.** 1929

Barney, Natalie Clifford. **Traits et Portraits.** 1963

Brooks, Romaine. **Portraits, Tableaux, Dessins.** 1952

Carpenter, Edward. **Intermediate Types Among Primitive Folk.** 1919

Casal, Mary. **The Stone Wall.** 1930

Cory, Donald Webster. **The Homosexual in America.** 1951

Craigin, Elisabeth. **Either Is Love.** 1937

Daughters of Bilitis. **The Ladder.** Volumes I - XVI. Including an **Index To The Ladder** by Gene Damon. 1956 - 1972. Nine vols.

Documents of the Homosexual Rights Movement in Germany, 1836 - 1927. 1975

Ellis, Havelock and John Addington Symonds. **Sexual Inversion.** 1897

Fitzroy, A. T. **Despised and Rejected.** 1917

Ford, Charles and Parker Tyler. **The Young and Evil.** 1933

Frederics, Diana. **Diana: A Strange Autobiography.** 1939

Friedlaender, Benedict. **Renaissance des Eros Uranios.** 1904

A Gay Bibliography. 1975

A Gay News Chronology, 1969 - May, 1975. 1975

Gordon, Mary. **Chase of the Wild Goose.** 1936

Government Versus Homosexuals. 1975

Grosskurth, Phyllis. **John Addington Symonds.** 1964

Gunn, Peter. **Vernon Lee: Violet Paget, 1856 - 1935.** 1964

A Homosexual Emancipation Miscellany, c. 1835 - 1952. 1975

Karsch-Haack, F[erdinand]. **Das Gleichgeschlechtliche Leben der Naturvölker.** 1911

Katz, Jonathan. **Coming Out!** 1975

Lesbianism and Feminism in Germany, 1895 - 1910. 1975

Lind, Earl. **Autobiography of an Androgyne.** 1918

Lind, Earl. **The Female-Impersonators.** 1922

Loeffler, Donald L. **An Analysis of the Treatment of the Homosexual Character in Dramas Produced in the New York Theatre From 1950 to 1968.** 1975

Mallet, Françoise. **The Illusionist.** 1952

Miss Marianne Woods and Miss Jane Pirie Against Dame Helen Cumming Gordon. 1811 - 1819

Mattachine Society. **Mattachine Review.** Volumes I - XIII. 1955 - 1966. Six vols.

Mayne, Xavier. **Imre: A Memorandum.** 1908

Mayne, Xavier. **The Intersexes.** 1908

Morgan, Claire. **The Price of Salt.** 1952

Niles, Blair. **Strange Brother.** 1931

Olivia. **Olivia.** 1949

Rule, Jane. **The Desert of the Heart.** 1964

Sagarin, Edward. **Structure and Ideology in an Association of Deviants.** 1975

Steakley, James D. **The Homosexual Emancipation Movement in Germany.** 1975

Sturgeon, Mary C. **Michael Field.** 1921

Sutherland, Alistair and Patrick Anderson. **Eros: An Anthology of Friendship.** 1961

Sweet, Roxanna Thayer. **Political and Social Action in Homophile Organizations.** 1975

Tobin, Kay and Randy Wicker. **The Gay Crusaders.** 1972

Ulrichs, Carl Heinrich. **Forschungen Über Das Rätsel Der Mannmännlichen Liebe.** 1898

Underwood, Reginald. **Bachelor's Hall.** 1937

[Vincenzo], Una, Lady Troubridge. **The Life of Radclyffe Hall.** 1963

Vivien, Renée **Poèmes de Renée Vivien.** Two vols. in one. 1923/24

Weirauch, Anna Elisabet. **The Outcast.** 1933

Weirauch, Anna Elisabet. **The Scorpion.** 1932

Wilhelm, Gale. **Torchlight to Valhalla.** 1938

Wilhelm, Gale. **We Too Are Drifting.** 1935

Winsloe, Christa. **The Child Manuela.** 1933